W9-CKM-788

CONNECTING

CONNECTING

Healing for Ourselves and Our Relationships
A Radical New Vision

LARRY CRABB

WORD PUBLISHING
Nashville·London·Vancouver·Melbourne

PUBLISHED BY WORD PUBLISHING
Nashville, Tennessee

Unless otherwise indicated,
Scripture quotations used in this book are
from the Holy Bible, New International Version (NIV).
Copyright © 1973, 1978, 1984 International Bible Society.
Used by permission of Zondervan Bible Publishers.

Scriptures marked RSV are from the Revised Standard Version
of the Bible. Copyright © 1946, 1952, 1971, 1973 by the Division of
Christian Education of the National Council of the Churches
of Christ in the U.S.A., and are used by permission.

Published in association with Sealy M. Yates,
Literary Agent, Orange, California.

LIBRARY OF CONGRESS CATALOGING-IN-PUBLICATION DATA
Crabb, Lawrence, J.
Connecting: healing for ourselves and our relationships
a radical new vision / Larry Crabb.
p.   cm.
ISBN 0-8499-1413-2
1. Interpersonal relations—Religious aspects—Christianity.
I. Title.
BV4597.52.C7   1997
248.4—dc21
97-26524
CIP

Printed in the United States of America
8 9 0 1 2 3 4 BVG 9 8 7 6 5 4 3 2

To the
Symphony Sunday School Class
at Foothills Bible Church
A Connecting Community

CONTENTS

ACKNOWLEDGMENTS

I've walked through high winds and rain many times, but this book was written during a hurricane. Without the support of many, it would have never been completed.

- Our team of friends committed to praying for Rachael and me throughout this writing project: Hank and Lil Bradicich, Chuck and Judy Yeager, Phoebe Crabb, Kent and Karla Denlinger, Bill and Sandy Welbon, Dave and Jeanni Shepherd, Frank and Chris Wilson, Linda Williams, Christine Campbell, Carole Novak, Anthony and Diane Vartuli, Ken and Carolyn Crabb, Deb Synnott, Trip and Judy Moore, Bob and Claudia Ingram, Bonnie Schry, Jim and Suzi Kallam, Richard and Lindsay Brown, Randy and Marcia Hinds, Kep and Kim Crabb.

- "Feedback friends" who gave several evenings to offer reactions to the manuscript: Bruce Marler, Duncan Sprague, Gary Hein, Doug Barker, Al Stirling, Milt Bryan, Scott Sawyer, Ferdinand Feliciano, Helene Ashker, Evan Morgan, Tom Board.

- The team at Word who believed in this book and in me: Kip Jordon, Joey Paul, Laura Kendall, and so many others.

All were anchors in this storm.

Two more people must be given special thanks:

Sealy: A man who, as few others, prays for me.

Claudia: Your servant spirit prevents you from knowing all that you mean to Rachael and me. Thanks for *everything!*

Rachael: Never has the gold of your character shone more brightly than during these difficult days. You're the most remarkable woman I know.

INTRODUCTION:

A Shift in My Thinking

Writing this book feels more like a surprising adventure than a predictable "next effort" in my literary career. It is not a book that I intended to write five years ago.

But what I am now writing reflects some fuzzy thinking that has been hanging around the corners of my mind for a long time, thinking that has recently climbed to center stage and gained a compellingly clear focus. After a quarter century of puzzling over people's problems and wondering how a psychologist could help, I have been captured by an idea that is moving me away from familiar ground toward large fields of uncharted territory.

The idea is this: When two people *connect,* when their beings intersect as closely as two bodies during intercourse, something is poured out of one and into the other that has the power to heal the soul of its deepest wounds and restore it to health. The one who receives experiences the joy of being healed. The one who gives knows the even greater joy of being used to heal. Something good is in the heart of each of God's children that is more powerful than everything bad. It's there, waiting to be released, to work its magic. But it rarely happens.

For a surgeon to abandon a practice in order to study nutrition would, at first glance, seem an unreasonable thing to do. Why not continue with the legitimate work of surgery, a proven means of doing considerable good that only a select group of highly trained professionals can perform?

The shift would make little sense, *unless* the doctor had strong reason to suspect that improved eating habits could actually reverse disease more powerfully and quickly than surgery. Then, by studying nutrition, the surgeon would be working toward the day when invasive, hard-to-schedule operations would no longer be necessary, when vegetables, not scalpels, would do the job.

In recent days, I have made a shift. I am now working toward the day when communities of God's people, ordinary Christians whose lives regularly intersect, will accomplish most of the good that we now depend on mental health professionals to provide. And they will do it by *connecting* with each other in ways that only the gospel makes possible.

Imagine what could happen if God were to place within his people intangible nutrients that had the power to both prevent and reverse soul disease and then told us to share those nutrients with each other in a special kind of intimate relating called connection. Imagine what could happen if that were true, if we believed it, and if we devoted ourselves to understanding what those nutrients were and how we could give them away.

I hope to demonstrate that that is exactly what God has done. He has deposited within us an energy that can heal soul disease, a power that is released to do its miraculous work as we relate in certain ways with each other. Our difficulty is that we don't believe it and therefore haven't thought much about it. But that could change.

I envision a community of people who intentionally mingle in settings where these nutrients are passed back and forth, where I pour into you the healing resources within me and you pour into me what God has put in you. Like spiritual gifts, these nutrients only nourish our own souls as we give them away for the blessing of others.

But what are they? What do I have within me that could deeply impact your life? How do I get them into you? And what is required of me to receive them from you and of you to give them to me? What does it mean to connect with other people in a way that forms healing community?

For the last twenty-five years, I have been practicing a form of surgery. As a professional therapist, I have removed the diagnosed patient from his or her natural setting; I have offered myself as a credentialed specialist to do what we all assume nonprofessionals cannot do and therefore should never attempt; and I have entered into private, vital parts of the patient's life that are rarely seen, let alone adequately dealt with, outside a therapist's office. During the last fourteen of those twenty-five years, I have trained other people to provide similar services.

I look back on all that time with great satisfaction. By any standard, I have enjoyed success in my professional career and have helped some folks along the way. It would make obvious good sense to keep on the same track for the next twenty-five years.

But that's not what I'm doing. I have strong reason to suspect that Christians sitting dutifully in church congregations, for whom "going to church" means doing a variety of spiritual activities, have been given resources that if released could powerfully heal broken hearts, overcome the damage done by abusive backgrounds, encourage the depressed to courageously move forward, stimulate the lonely to reach out, revitalize discouraged teens and children with new and holy energy, and introduce hope into the lives of the countless people who feel rejected, alone, and useless. Maybe "going to church," more than anything else, means relating to several people in your life differently. *Maybe the center of Christian community is connecting with a few.*

I want to see people connect with a few others as intimately as the various parts of my body work together, as cooperatively as my fingers are working together to write these words. With blood from one heart flowing through each finger and instructions from one mind controlling their movement, the job gets done. If one finger were to suffer a cut, my body would quickly send life-giving resources to the damage site to fight off infection and help restore the finger to full use.

The church, we're told on good authority, is ". . . held together by every supporting ligament." Does that mean that a church community can hold me together when my life is falling apart? The church is designed to "grow and build itself up in love, as each part does its work" (Eph. 4:15–16).

But what does that mean? What does a community of a connected few look like? Will it happen through the good activities that for most people define church life? Can we go on relating to our family and friends as we have and expect it to happen? Or is something more needed?

I suggest that it's time to take a hard look at what really gets passed back and forth in our relationships and to ask what is being withheld that, if given, could change our lives. It's time to consider a radical understanding of "going to church" that centers on releasing the power to change lives that God has placed within every member of the Christian community, a community Christ calls his body, a community made up of lots of people connecting to a few others.

What would it mean to enter the battle for someone else's soul by connecting with them? Does soul care deal with the core issues lying beneath a history of sexual abuse? Does connection address what's going on beneath panic attacks, shoplifting, and eating disorders? Is there real power to do what needs to be done in ordinary relationships?

When Paul proclaimed Christ "so that we may present everyone perfect," was he grappling with what we moderns call emotional problems? When he claimed that the energy of Christ was powerfully working through him as he related to others, was it an energy that might help a parent worried sick over a rebellious drug-abusing son or a troubled eating-disordered daughter? When he felt as though he were in the pains of childbirth until Christ was formed in the lives of people he loved, was something coming out of him that could meaningfully help a woman struggling with multiple personalities or a man who has never felt close to anyone?

I have been captured by the idea that God has placed extraordinary resources within us that have the power to heal us and our relationships. If released they could do a lot of good that we now think only trained specialists can accomplish. I believe that, under the direction of the Holy Spirit, these resources can do whatever needs to be done to move people toward maturity. I have what it takes, not as a psychologist but as a Christian husband, to help my wife become deeply whole. I can influence my kids, help my friends, and be an instrument of soul healing in the lives of a few. The core requirement is that I be godly. It's easier to get educated.

I envision the church as people who are connected in small healing communities, connected by what they give to each other. Perhaps they gather with other little communities in larger groups to celebrate the life they share and be instructed in that life and then go out to connect even more deeply and invite others to enjoy that same intimacy.

Introduction

My burden is twofold:

1. To understand the Christian life (and those who want to live it) in a way that frees us to release the good that God has placed within us. I want to move away from the pressure to live up to a set of pre-scribed standards, and I don't want to keep trying to repair what-ever damage our backgrounds may have caused.

2. To understand what community could be in a way that excites us with its potential to liberate, strengthen, and encourage just a few and to touch the deepest, deadest, most terrifying parts of those people's souls with resurrection power.

Beneath these two burdens is a longing to understand the gospel of Jesus Christ in a way that fills us with passionate confidence that it can do what no other force in heaven or earth can do. Throughout the book, I assume the gospel is the good news that believing that Jesus is the Christ guarantees eternal life to the believer (John 20:31). Believing the truth about Jesus, that he is God in the flesh, that he died to pay the price for our sins, and that he freely forgives everyone who believes that he is who he says he is and that he does what he says he does, is saving faith.

And with saving faith comes the gift of life. As I will later make clear, that gift means more than forgiveness and a guaranteed future. It also means that I now possess the life of Christ, the same energy that was released in everything he did, most visibly in how he related. When I realize the gospel has equipped me to relate with that energy, I get excited about what Christ could do through my life as I enter into other people's lives.

As we progress in our understanding of these things, my prayer is that "going to church" will become the most important activity in our lives, the activity of building healing communities of a connected few.

MY MIDLIFE CRISIS

A few years back I turned fifty. The reflection required of folks who reach that milestone led me to realize something was missing. It dawned on me that I had somehow survived half a century without going through a full-fledged, dream-shattering, midlife crisis, and that felt wrong, or at least unfashionable.

So I prayed about it. And God was faithful. He answered exceedingly abundantly.

After more than twenty-five years as a psychologist, about half in practice and half teaching, I have reached a few conclusions that have required me to shift the focus of my work. The conclusions don't feel entirely new, just more central. Let me express them this way.

- *Beneath what our culture calls psychological disorder is a soul crying out for what only community can provide.* There is no "disorder" requiring "treatment." And, contrary to hard-line moralism, there is more to our struggles than a stubborn will needing firm admonishment. Beneath all our problems, there are desperately hurting souls that must find the nourishment only community can provide—or die.

- *We must do something other than train professional experts to fix damaged psyches. Damaged psyches aren't the problem. The problem beneath our struggles is a disconnected soul.* And we must do something more than exhort people to do what's right and then hold them accountable. Groups tend to emphasize accountability when they don't know how to relate. Better behavior through exhortation isn't the solution, though it sometimes is part of it. Rather than fixing psyches or scolding sinners, we must provide nourishment for the disconnected soul that only a community of connected people can offer.

  The crisis of care in modern culture, especially in the Western church, will not be resolved by training more therapists. We do not need a counseling center on every corner. It will be worsened by moralists who never reach deeply into the hearts of people in their efforts to impose their standards of behavior on others, even when those standards are biblical.*

---

* Some readers may be interested in the implications of my thinking for professional counseling, especially for Christian counseling. In Appendix A, I refer to recent research in psychotherapy to argue that the considerable good done by trained counselors could,

Introduction

• *The greatest need in modern civilization is the development of communities—true communities where the heart of God is home, where the humble and wise learn to shepherd those on the path behind them, where trusting strugglers lock arms with others as together they journey on.*

As I have shared these conclusions at conferences and in a few publications, I have lost students and disturbed friends and raised more than a few eyebrows. I fear, too, I have made a few friends I will not keep.

But I have been most surprised (and gratified) by the number of people who have said, "You're on the right track. Keep going." One psychiatrist wrote to tell me I was committing professional suicide. And then he added, "And it's about time!"

I think so too. It's about time to go beneath the moralism that assumes the church's job is done when it instructs people in biblical principles and then exhorts them to do right. It's about time to find a better way to help each other when we struggle than the way of our therapeutic culture, which looks beneath every troublesome emotion or behavior pattern to find a psychological disorder that needs repair.

It's about time to free ourselves from the pressure that moralism creates and to tone down our preoccupying fascination with our internal workings, whether with psychological dynamics or with the subtleties of idolatry, a fascination that therapy often encourages.

I want us to think about the kind of connection that is required for a small group of people, perhaps a family or a couple of friends, to become a healing community. I want to understand how a father can relate to a sullen, troubled son with a power that could change his direction. I want to be able to guide the wife of an angry husband toward a path that could restore their relationship.

---

in many cases, be done as well or better by mature, nonprofessionally qualified people who relate well. I provide a quick overview of the development of the "talking cure" to bolster my point.

Then, in Appendix B, I sketch my understanding of when professional help is appropriate, and suggest the kind of resources that a community could develop to deal with the vast majority of personal concerns. If these topics are of interest, I suggest reading both appendices before proceeding with chapter 1.

I want us to be honest about the insecurities, fears, and inadequacies that lie hidden in our hearts, beneath the appearances we may present to others. I want us to speak with neither shame nor pride about the dark nights of our soul. I want us to be able to tell the stories of our abuse, rejection, or failure to a few special people who will listen and know they can't take the pain away, to people who will not think something is wrong with us that a therapist can fix and who will not simply tell us to get a grip on things.

But I don't want us to focus on the hard things, the ugly things, the awful things. I don't want us to gloss over them—we must never pretend that things are better than they are—but I do want us to look beneath all that is difficult and see the miracle God has wrought in our hearts.

I want us to see that he has placed powerful urges to do good in the deepest recesses of our regenerated hearts. That's what the New Covenant is all about. Something wonderful and beautiful and resilient is within us that no abuse, rejection, or failure can ever destroy. I want us to focus on that!

A friend of mine spent a weekend with a Christian ministry for troubled young people. During a morning session of the residents and their parents, a young woman rose to address the group.

With trembling lips and tears of shame streaming down her face, she said, "I've been a prostitute for the last three years. I am so sorry."

As she stood there, paralyzed by her vulnerability, her father left his seat, walked to the front of the room, embraced the shaking girl, and said, "When I look at you, I see no prostitute in you. You've been washed. I see my beautiful daughter."

She replied, "I had forgotten the joy of being your little girl."

I want us to relate to one another, not as moralist to sinner or therapist to patient, but as saint to saint, father to child, friend to friend, as true lovers, with the confidence that we can help each other believe that, by the grace of God, there is something good beneath the mess. Even when all we can see is the mess, I want us to believe that we can nourish the good and encourage its release.

This book is a call to *healing relationships,* a call away from a moralism that thinks the law is still outside of us and that we need to be pressured to obey it, a call away from the assumption that professional training equips people better than godliness to speak powerfully into people's lives. This is a call toward the day when our deepest wounds and struggles will be meaningfully and adequately dealt with in the ordinary relationships of life.

God has given us the power to be his instrument in healing souls. That power is waiting to be released.

I am writing to ordinary people, to dads and moms, husbands and wives, friends and colleagues, to everyone who understands that we cannot make it on our own, that we cannot become all we could be without the love, wisdom, and feedback of others. I am writing to anyone who yearns to escape the miseries of loneliness and a meaningless existence by richly connecting with at least a few other people but perhaps isn't sure how to go about it.

I am writing to folks who sincerely want to make a positive difference in the lives of the people they love but who feel inadequate to do so. Exactly how do you connect with an angry or depressed spouse or with a shy child who hides in her room while the neighborhood kids play together? How do you connect with someone you just don't like or someone who has hurt you? How do you move connectingly toward others when you feel insecure, afraid you'll not be wanted? How do you help a friend who worries too much or a daughter who won't communicate?

I am writing to that middle-aged couple who sees a younger couple struggling and wants to help but isn't sure how, to the father of an estranged adult son whose every overture is rebuffed, to the friend of a busy person who feels close to no one but acts the part of a well-adjusted, together woman.

When you finish reading this book, I think you will have a new understanding of what you can give to others and how you can make a powerful difference in their lives and in your own.

My discussion begins with a story about my older son who was lifted out of significant struggle by the power of connecting. It continues as I spell out the three ingredients of healing community and then illustrate their power in the life of a well-known spiritual leader (chapters 1 through 3).

I then explore why connecting is so powerful and why alternative ways of helping don't accomplish nearly as much. We are all disconnected people, and it is the unbearable reality of separateness that causes us so many problems. My central point in chapters 3 through 7 is that the gospel of Christ connects us to God, to ourselves, and to others; it places something alive and wonderful in our forgiven hearts that bridges the gap of separateness and joins us in life-bearing union. We now have something to give that has the power to change the entire course of someone else's existence.

Chapters 8 through 14 ask some important questions: Why is real connection so rare? What gets in the way? Why do we settle for counterfeit connection, for a false intimacy that changes no one? And what can we do about it? What must we do to clear away the obstacles to what we really want?

In chapters 15 through 18, I suggest a game plan for relating powerfully to others, for dreaming good dreams about what we could become, and for helping one another get there.

CHAPTER 1

The clock on the back wall of the hotel conference room announced it was 9 P.M., exactly. I closed the session in prayer and stepped down from the platform.

It was Thursday evening. The week-long seminar, a day and a half from ending, was going well.

As I left the auditorium, I remember feeling powerful. I was teaching well. The audience was attentive. Several had expressed what God was doing in their hearts through the teaching. I felt good.

Our habit was to grab a light snack in the hotel restaurant before turning in. As my colleague and I reached the elevator, Dan pressed the button that would take us to our floor. "We're not going to the restaurant," he announced.

"Why not?" I objected. "I'm hungry. I want something to eat."

"I'll tell you why when we get there, but you and I are going to the room." It didn't require much discernment to realize something was wrong.

"Sit down," he instructed a few minutes later. He then took a deep breath and as gently as he could said, "Rachael phoned while you were speaking tonight. Kep has been expelled from Taylor. She wants you to call."

Three short sentences. Knife thrusts into my heart.

Kep, our older son, twenty, was nearing the end of the first semester of his junior year at Taylor University. Ken, seventeen, was on the same campus beginning his freshman year.

1

When Kep was born, I gave him to the Lord and vowed to do my part in steering him in good directions, to fill his mind with the truth of God. I prayed the same prayer two and a half years later when Ken arrived. No parent worked harder to do it right: prayers every night; stories with a Christian point before they went to sleep; Saturdays given over to swim meets; afternoons to basketball games and karate lessons; annual father-son birthday meals (at the restaurant of his choice) when I asked each boy the same twelve questions, recorded his answers, and discussed them at the next year's birthday meal as a way of exploring development; a special thirteenth birthday trip with each son to introduce him to adolescence, complete with illustrated lectures on the birds and bees; return trips to the same fun spot on their twenty-first birthdays to launch them into adulthood.

When our boys were six and eight, I bought an overhead projector for family devotions. (How many dads have done *that?*) Old Testament survey, New Testament survey, basic theology, book studies—we did it all. Discipline was consistent, including spankings followed by hugs and prayers. *What went wrong? What didn't I do?*

There was no lack of fun times. I once built a stand for Ken to sell a hot dog and lemonade lunch for fifty cents. He made twenty-one dollars. I spent thirty-seven.

When Kep showed the first signs of clear rebellion, I recall screaming at God: "What else do you want me to do? I've done everything I know!"

I also screamed at my wife. We were driving out of the parking lot of the Warsaw Health Food Store on Center Street when Rachael said, "Kep has his SAT exam tomorrow. What do you think he's doing right now in the parking lot outside the basketball game?" I pounded my fist on the dashboard of our car and yelled, "Why can't you let up on him?" She later told me that she felt blamed for all the trouble. Her words: "You made me feel that it was all my fault because I gave birth to him."

I hurt my wife. Badly. That kind of pain doesn't easily disappear. What words could I say, what deeds could I do that would have the power to soothe that pain, to touch the deepest part of her soul with healing love? How does a husband connect with a wife he has damaged?

During Kep's most difficult years, from fourteen to twenty, I grounded him, prayed for him, prayed with him, took long walks with him, bought him a car that I later sold as punishment. I remember using the well-worn line of frustrated parents: "I will not tolerate this kind of behavior while you are living under my roof." When he was eighteen, I told him that unless he committed himself to living by my standards (which I represented as God's), I would give him one hundred dollars and require him to leave our home.

I told him I loved him, I listened to him when he wanted to talk, I made firm decisions after taking his perspective into account, trying to give latitude wherever I could. I did everything I knew to do. Nothing reached him.

I know of nothing more agonizing than watching someone you love moving in a bad direction and feeling absolutely powerless to do anything about it.

What else could I have done? *What else could I have done?*

When he began his third year at Taylor, I purchased a small home on the outskirts of the campus for Kep to move into with several of his friends. Rachael and I helped clean the dirty floors and cabinets, cut the weeds so they resembled a lawn, and shopped garage sales for sofas, beds, and desks.

I had such good dreams. My son would get involved in spiritual leadership on campus, the home would be a gathering spot for Bible studies, Kep would meet a wonderful Christian girl, take her to Ivanhoe's for ice cream after bonfire rallies before big games, and graduate with a bright future and a beautiful fiancée.

Maybe I was dreaming the wrong dreams.

But they seemed so right. I knew exactly what my son should become. I had no thought of *releasing* him, I wanted only to *control* him, to reduce him to someone predictable. I had my dreams. I'll never forget the time he turned to me during his last year of high school and said, with fury in every word, "You couldn't bear the thought of your son not going to college."

It was in that off-campus college home that Kep got into real trouble. And now he was expelled.

I called Rachael. I called Kep. I called the airlines. The first flight available was the next afternoon. I laid on my bed, decided to go ahead and present the Friday morning lecture—it was on parenting—and then reflected on what I was facing.

The first of two profoundly strange experiences happened that Thursday night. As I lay on the bed, I was overwhelmed by the phrase, "This is an opportunity." Dan asked how I was feeling. I replied, "Calm. Something's going on that's bigger than me, but I'm a part of it." I didn't cry. I slept well.

The next morning, after giving my lecture (that was difficult), I flew home. Rachael and I held each other and cried. But they were not tears of despair. We sensed this was an opportunity that God intended to seize.

The closeness we felt bridged some of the emotional gap between us. But not nearly all of it. There was still much work to do. Healing takes time. And because I didn't know how to release what was in me that could heal my wife's soul, the healing took too much time. It still continues, as it will in all of us till we're home.

I drove the hour and a half trip to Taylor through open fields of Indiana farmland on quiet country roads. God was near. I talked with him as if he were sitting in the passenger seat. "Lord, I've done everything I know to do. I've not reached my son. And I can't reach him now. I don't know how to do it. But I'm not asking for instructions. I'm asking you to let him see Christ in me. Nothing will change him but a taste of what his heart most deeply wants. Principles, insights, rebukes just won't do it. He needs to meet you. Give yourself to him through me, please!"

When I greeted Kep, the second strange experience took place. I wasn't angry! *I really wasn't angry!* I didn't have to control my temper or watch my words. Something from deep within me poured out toward my son through unremarkable words. I simply said, "How can I help?"

I recently discussed the happenings of that time with my younger son. Ken said, "I remember how mad you were when Kep got into trouble in high school. You wouldn't talk to anyone for weeks. That was the hardest thing for me. But I watched the way you handled Kep when he was kicked out of Taylor. It was different. And I felt included."

It was within the next few days that the prodigal came home. And I mean far more than the fact that Kep returned to our house. Here's how

Kep recently expressed it: "I did come back to the Lord during that time, but first I came back to you."

The father who so many times before *demanded* repentance angrily, manipulatively, self-dependently, now *invited* repentance. Kep's heart turned away from pleasures that left him empty and turned toward something better, something that didn't merely numb the ache in his soul but actually touched it. He felt the hope that he might know the joy of being wanted, accepted, liked, of having someone believe that he had something to give that could impact others with delight.

That was a turning point in Kep's life. Why? What happened? Something came out of Jesus to heal the woman with the issue of blood. Something came out of me that cut through Kep's hardness and reached the tender part of his soul with healing power. Could that really be true? If so, what was it?

For years I had been so powerless. Why? Was it God's sovereign plan to reach my son at that time? Of course. Had I learned the secret of releasing power earlier, would our family have been spared the heartache of rebellion? I don't know.

But one thing I do know: *A power was released through me that had never been as fully released before.*

Could it happen in your relationships? What would it take to release the power God has placed in your heart toward just one other person in your life? Perhaps a distant, cold wife that you've not been able to reach? Maybe a neglecting husband who thinks he's loving you well and hasn't a clue that your heart is aching for something more, something different. It might be a son or daughter who has trouble making friends, a teenager who won't communicate, an adult child who has sealed her heart so you cannot touch it. Or it could be a friend, a person you know is struggling.

Releasing the power of God through our lives into the hearts and souls of others requires that we both *understand* and *enter into* a kind of relating that only the gospel makes possible, a kind of relating that I call *connecting*. This kind of relating depends entirely on deep fellowship with Christ and then spills over on to other people with the power to change their lives, not always on our timetable or in the ways we expect but as the sovereign Spirit moves.

The story I've told about Kep happened in 1988. The work God began in his heart during those difficult days has continued. He is married to the woman we've prayed for since the day he was born, a beautiful godly young lady who is everything we hoped for and more. He works hard; he wants God's will for his life; he is involved in an excellent church. The miracle of the New Covenant has taken place: His heart is inclined toward God.

Only two things have ever changed the human soul: the *fall* and *grace*, the power of Satan and the power of God. And God is infinitely more powerful. Nothing is stronger than grace. Satan doesn't have any. God is defined by it.

Kep's life was changed. So was Ken's. Mine was too. And Rachael's. But so much more change is needed.

There is a power within the life of every Christian waiting to be released, a power that could lead to further and deeper change, a power within you that could help someone else connect more intimately to the heart of Christ.

We haven't yet dreamed big enough dreams of what we could mean to one another. Maybe it's time.

CHAPTER 2

Three Ingredients of Healing Community

For more than twenty-five years, my burden has been to help people change. During that time, I've developed a reputation as an effective counselor. I am profoundly grateful that many people report that I've been a meaningful part of their movement toward greater joy and freedom. Happily, I believe them.

But for a long time I've sensed something missing, both in my understanding of how to help others and in my efforts to apply that understanding to my own life. Of course, I expect to step into my grave saying the same thing—something will *always* be missing in our grasp of truth till we get home—but the insistent awareness of gaps that nudges us to keep moving on our journey should not be ignored.

A former student recently said, "I watch my neighbor jog every day, bicycle to a Rockies game, fly a kite with his kids, and wash his car on Saturday mornings—and I wonder about my own life. Here I am, enlightened enough to ponder things so deeply that I explore tensions with my wife while Jim and his wife jog by on their way to the park. Jim is your basic nominal churchgoer. I read Psalm 73 to convince myself that I'm on to something and he's not. But sometimes I wonder."

With my tongue only partly pressed against my cheek, I reacted, "Maybe Jim has it more right than we do." Frankly, I'm a bit weary of the focus on struggle. Do we Western Christians, so pampered by the comforts of modern civilization, sometimes glorify struggle and wear trials like merit badges rather than joyfully pursuing the good things of God and rejoicing when we're "counted worthy of suffering disgrace for the Name"? (Acts 5:41). Are we trying to recover some passion in our lives by talking so much about our problems?

Maybe there is something to enjoy about being Christian that is deeply passionate, something so good that we really can regard our struggles as unworthy of comparison not only with what lies ahead but also with the glory of our journey in that direction. Maybe the key has much to do with companionship on the journey, with a certain kind of community that bands together to scale the rugged peaks.

Every occupation has its own hazards. I'm a clinical psychologist, a professionally licensed therapist. A hazard of my job involves people's expectations that if I am truly competent to help others change in good ways, certainly my own life should reflect the fruit of that competence. It's difficult to take seriously a fat man extolling the virtues of the newest foolproof approach to weight loss.

The question beats against my conscience: Do I know the good so intimately that I gladly endure whatever hardship lies on the path to more of it? Do I know how to share that good with others?

As part of my postfifty reflections, I've had to admit that I still struggle with a lot of the same problems people pay me to help them deal with. That's not a new thought, but it strikes with more force today than it did ten or twenty years ago. I thought I'd be farther along the path toward maturity than I perceive myself to be.

And, to add another wrinkle to an already well-creased puzzle, I've noticed that whatever maturity I can claim seems to have come about through the influence of factors that I may not have always placed at the center of my efforts to help others.

For the most part, I've been a "figure-things-out-expose-what's-wrong-then-make-appropriate-corrections" type of counselor. Give me a problem, and I go to work. Panic attacks? I'll help you find the deeper fears you've never faced and work them through. Addiction problems? It may take a while, but I'll root out your idolatrous demand for reliable pleasure and your hatred for an unmanageable God, then I'll guide you on a journey through terrified self-dependence toward vigorous trust.

When it's time, I'll throw in a healthy dash of instruction, some generous tablespoons of advice and exhortation, then I'll let things simmer for a while under my watchful eye of accountability. Like most counselors, churches, and families, I depend on the tried-and-true approaches of fix-what's-wrong and do-what's-right to promote good change in others.

But the result has not always been what I'd hoped for, either in myself or others. Too many victims of self-focused therapy and pressuring moralism sit in their living rooms fussing about either the deep or bad things in their lives while Jim and his wife jog to the park, in good enough aerobic shape to chat happily while they run.

No doubt some Jims are fiddling while their homes burn to the ground, Nero-style, but a few are soaring on wings like eagles, running along with renewed strength, and walking through deep valleys without growing faint (Isaiah 40:31).

I want that for my wife, my two sons, my two daughters-in-law, my friends, my clients, myself. I'm convinced I won't help you or me get there by merely understanding problems ("sounds to me like a passive-aggressive reaction") or exhorting worthy change ("you need to take responsibility for yourself").

But, in a nutshell, that's what I've been depending on to promote change. Certainly I've emphasized the need to trust God, to know him, to surrender ourselves to him, to quit trying to explain him, to immerse ourselves in his Word, but, like most Christians, I've put a great deal of stock in self-awareness and self-discipline. Know yourself and choose wisely. And that's pretty good advice.

It's become clear to me, though, that God handles things a bit differently. He does, of course, rebuke and exhort, and his Spirit does search our hearts for hidden matters that interfere with trust. *But the absolute center of what he does to help us change is to reveal himself to us, to give us a taste of what he's really like, and to pour his life into us.* And a critical element in the revealing process is to place us in a community of people who are enough like him to give us that taste firsthand. If that is true, if a powerful experience of God comes through others, then connecting plays a vital, indispensable, powerful role in effectively addressing the core issues of our souls, the issues that lie beneath all our personal, emotional, and psychological problems.

God no longer stands in front of us, drill-sergeant style, barking orders. He is now inside us, whispering with attractive authority that it's time to hit the deck and do fifty push-ups. And now we want to do it, not because the activity itself is fun, but because it fits our nature (we're soldiers) and we enjoy pleasing our commander (we love him).

Neither does God tinker with our old nature, that tangled system of God-doubting, self-protective, pain-denying passions within us that the Bible calls our *flesh*. Rather than entering the dark places of our souls with a flashlight and a scalpel, intent on repairing what's wrong, he enters with a flashlight and a smile, eager to let us see how he feels about us even when we stand exposed in his presence.

God's method is neither to merely issue commands from the general's tent (do what's right) nor to improve the functioning of diseased organs (fix what's wrong). Instead he becomes so intimately a part of us that we want to resist whatever he doesn't like and release the good things he has aroused within us.

The most powerful thing we can do to help someone change is to offer them a rich taste of God's incredible goodness in the New Covenant. He looks at us with eyes of delight, with eyes that see a goodness beneath the mess, with a heart that beats wildly with excitement over who we are and who we will become. And sometimes he exposes what we are convinced would make him turn away in disgust in order to amaze us with his grace. That's connecting. When we connect like that, it can change people's lives.

God doesn't fix us or pressure us. He does whatever it takes to reveal himself to us. That may include probing deeply into our messy hearts or insisting we do something we really don't want to do. But the core purpose is always the same, not to repair or exhort us, but to draw us into a fuller appreciation of his beauty, to dazzle us with the sunrises of his nature, to awe us with the Grand Canyons of his character, to entice us with the endless fields of fragrant flowers blooming in his heart.

Let me shift from poetic expression to an outline, complete with brief annotations. God helps us become more like Christ by doing three things:

First, he provides us a taste of Christ delighting in us—*the essence of connection:*

- Accepting who we are

- Envisioning who we could be

Second, he diligently searches within us for the good he has put there—*an affirming exposure:*

- Remaining calm when badness is visible

- Keeping confidence that goodness lies beneath

Third, he engagingly exposes what is bad and painful—*a disruptive exposure:*

- Claiming the special opportunities to reveal grace that the difficult content of our hearts provide

Before in my counseling, I spent too much time with the flesh. I over-studied doubt, denial, self-preserving psychological dynamics, and our selfishly driven strategies for relating to people. These topics are worthy of serious investigation, but it's easy (and appealing to the flesh) to become more fascinated with these matters than we need to be and, in the process, less appreciative of the power available in experiencing Christ.

Looking back, I think I failed to emphasize that beneath all the bad is goodness, that a careful exploration of the redeemed heart does not sink us in a cesspool; it's more like mining for gold in a dirty cave. I relied on "interpretive wisdom," on my ability to see and surface the buried goals, beliefs, images, longings, and emotions within people's hearts, rather than on the spiritual character of my heart. I did not appreciate how powerfully the energy that carried my words to other people confirmed *either* their suspicion that God is more chess player than poet, more sergeant than lover, *or* that he is everything we could possibly imagine—and beyond.

Too, there was (and still is) something in me that *enjoyed* disrupting people with an exposure of how bad or hurting they were. It was, I think, less sadistic than it might sound and based more on the sense that when people were "stirred up," we were getting somewhere. It is easier to stir people deeply with their pain and struggle than with the good things within them. It felt like doing surgery while other folks, in the name of kindness, were merely applying Band-Aids.

But the point of disrupting folks with an exposure of what's wrong is to more fully reveal God's grace and to create a fuller appreciation for what that grace has done. When we look for the bad, we must always be looking harder for the hidden good.

Causing disruption through exposing internal darkness has its place. It is wrong to deny that darkness, but it is more wrong to become fascinated with it and stay there. "Encountering darkness in our lives should not drive us from prayer, but drive us to prayer." We help each other face the hard parts in our lives in order to realize there is a greater power. "Our trust in God" in the midst of facing darkness "is a realization that he is already working for, in, and through us, calling us to a new, whole life beyond our broken lives."[1]

What I now believe was missing in my former approach to helping people was an appreciation of the power of connecting. In the remainder of this chapter, I want to briefly discuss the three elements that can make our relationships with those we love powerful. I want us to see that ordinary Christians, parents, spouses, friends have a power waiting to be released that could do significant things in other people's hearts. And that will take some work.

We typically feel impotent:

- "How can I help my wife with her depression? She needs more than I can give her."

- "My kid is a mess. I don't know what I'm doing. We need someone wise to tell us what to do."

- "I'm having lunch with a friend tomorrow. His wife just left him because she found out he has a sexual addiction. I can listen and I do care. But except for minor problems, that's just a Band-Aid. I don't do surgery."

- "I have no idea what my friend should do. He hates his job, is in serious debt, and is really discouraged. *I can't help!*"

But maybe you can. *To whatever degree you offer people these three ingredients, you will have a powerful impact on their lives.*

ELEMENT #1. A TASTE OF CHRIST DELIGHTING IN US

Why do we so infrequently delight in one another? It's people who don't know us well that often find the most to appreciate in us. And that leaves us worried that to know us is to *not* delight in us. Because we long to be delighted in, we keep friends at a distance from which they won't see the bad.

The problem, I think, is that we don't really believe there is something terrific in us that would arouse delight. Or, if there is, we believe that the *deeper* things, which are more true about us, are bad. Goodness lies on the surface. Badness runs deep. We're having a hard time believing the centerpiece of the New Covenant, *that forgiven people have caught a glimpse of Christ and that the Spirit has used that glimpse to create goodness within us,* a goodness that is more defining of who we are than our badness.

One of Satan's favorite strategies is to come up with a close counterfeit of an important truth and allow the Christian community to spot the error. Christians then become so committed to staying away from it that they miss the truth it distorted.

Humanism is a good example. Humanistic philosophy teaches that we're all essentially good, that goodness lies deeper in our beings than badness, that our badness reflects the corrupting power of bad environments. Christians rightly respond by insisting that in our natural selves dwells no goodness at all, that apart from Christ our best deeds are no more attractive than soiled rags. Before Christ, goodness is cosmetic, badness is defining.

We must stand firmly against humanistic error. But we must not stand so far away that we fail to appreciate the gospel truth that humanism counterfeits. In our flesh dwells no good thing, but Christians are more than flesh. We are now supernatural people, absolutely forgiven, clothed in Christ's spotless apparel, and gifted with a new heart brimming with wonderful desires to do good.

Remember an earlier sentence: The absolute center of what God does to help us change is to reveal himself to us. God loves to delight in people. But he could find no delight in us when all the inclinations of our hearts were continually evil, so he made us delightful. He gave us a new set of inclinations. Now, when we experience his delight, we're not puffed up with a proud version of self-esteem ("Aren't we something?"), nor do we react with self-contempt ("He can't really like me—I'm terrible."). We're grateful for what he's made us, given who we were and what we deserve ("Isn't he something? He really is *that* good!").

Good urges are *created* in us when we're forgiven. Good urges will completely *rule* in us when we see him and the belief of faith gives way to the excitement of sight. And good urges are *released* in us now as we get to know him better.

Until we realize that there are no legitimate longings in our souls beyond his power and intention to satisfy, all change is cosmetic. But as we grasp how tenderly committed he is to our well-being, we feel more inclined to obey. Good urges become stronger.

And God delights in the whole process. He delights in our status as forgiven children welcomed to the dining table, and he delights in what we will become as we eat more of the food he provides.

A friend of mine was raised in an angry family. Mealtimes were either silent or sarcastically noisy. Down the street was an old-fashioned house with a big porch where a happy family lived. My friend told me that when he was about ten, he began excusing himself from his dinner table as soon as he could without being yelled at and walking to the old-fashioned house down the street.

If he arrived during dinnertime, he would crawl under the porch and just sit there, listening to the sounds of laughter. When he told me this story, I asked him to imagine what it would have been like if the father in the house somehow knew he was huddled beneath the porch and sent his son to invite him in. I asked him to envision what it would have meant to him to accept the invitation, to sit at the table, to accidentally spill his glass of water, and hear the father roar with delight, "Get him more water! And a dry shirt. I want him to enjoy the meal!"

We need to hear the father laugh. Change depends on experiencing the character of God.

Until we thrill in the Father's embrace after admitting we've been prostitutes, until we watch him jump up and down with delight every time he sees us, until we hear him ask, "How can I help?" when we expected him to say "I'm sick and tired of putting up with you!" we will not change, not really, not consistently, not deeply.

Do we see the good in people, the good heart buried beneath all the pettiness and resentments and empire-building ambitions that irritate us so badly? Do we accept fellow Christians the way Christ accepts us, forgiving each other for the wrongs we do and believing there is something better?

Do we jump up and down with excitement over what someone else could become? How much time do we spend envisioning what that might be? Could we write a verbal portrait of what our rebellious son or estranged spouse or critical friend might look like in twenty years if God's Spirit has his way?

Without this foundational element of offering others a taste of Christ's delight in them, all our skillful techniques, our wise counsel, our insightful interpretations, even our warm encouragement, will add up to nothing. If there is no love, no supernatural delighting in who we are and who we one day will be, every effort to help people change will fall short of its potential.

ELEMENT #2. A DILIGENT SEARCH FOR WHAT IS GOOD

Someone has defined spiritual direction as recognizing what God is up to in someone's life and joining the process. But that doesn't describe what we typically do, either with ourselves or others, when we're troubled by a problem.

Take the common complaint of fatigue as an illustration. A friend makes known how tired he feels. He's been to the doctor. All tests are negative. The neighborhood herbalist has prescribed twenty or thirty pills a day. Maybe they're helping a bit.

Notice how our minds work in that situation. "I wonder what's wrong with this guy. I feel tired too. I've been worried that I have chronic fatigue syndrome. Maybe he should see a specialist, maybe a counselor. Could be he's depressed."

Whatever we verbalize, we usually include a series of questions ("Are you sleeping OK?" "How's your diet?"), a few suggestions ("We've been juicing at our home for a few months now. We think it's giving us more energy."), and some predictable sympathy ("Sounds tough. Hang in there. Hope you get to feeling better.").

Counselors often follow a more sophisticated version of the same procedure. They inquire to see if significant stress, anger, or guilt might be present; they suggest a regime of either extensively talking or changes in routine that might stimulate interest; and they offer support while their clients carry on.

For whatever reason, it doesn't come naturally to search for the good God may be releasing through this trial. If a medical problem is responsible for the fatigue, it needs to be found. If herbs will help, take them. I am not at all opposed to solving problems when solutions are available.

But a core ingredient of powerful impact is too easily overlooked in our search for solutions or our attempts at supportiveness. And that ingredient is an affirming exposure of whatever evidence of God's Spirit can be found in the midst of the problem.

Although there is a place for helping each other to see what God is teaching us through trials, that is not what I have in mind here. Rather than suggesting "Maybe God is teaching you patience through your battles with fatigue," I'd want to hear someone say, "It's amazing to me that you so clearly want to see your wife encouraged while you're feeling so bad. That really blesses me."

In a recent counseling session, Debbie snapped at her husband, "You tell me you feel judged by me. Well, let me tell you that's what I feel all the time. You're the most critical man I know. You never give me a break, and I'm tired of it!"

Picture yourself as her counselor, perhaps her friend or shepherd. Her husband Brad stares back at her in disgust. Debbie is trembling with rage. What do you say?

Do you point out her obvious anger: "You're feeling very alone and unappreciated."

Do you probe into the psychological roots of her strong emotions: "Where else have you felt so severely put down?"

Do you hold up biblical standards and exhort obedience: "Debbie, the Bible tells you to put aside anger. That's obviously hard to do, but it can—and must—be done."

Do you offer empathic support: "I know you feel very hurt by Brad right now. I hope you know how much I care and how much I believe in you."

If your disposition is to delight in Debbie with the passion of Christ and to thrill at the prospect of what she will one day become, then, with the essence of connecting in place, you will want to affirmingly expose the supernatural *integrity* within her and the good urges lying beneath her anger. Those urges are likely beyond her sight (and perhaps as weak and unformed as a week-old embryo).

With a heart that offers her a taste of how good God is, even at the moment of her anger, you might begin by affirming her awareness of what she most deeply longs for and her clear sense of right and wrong, both evidence of God's Spirit at work. "You not only want someone to deeply delight in you, but you would also love to give your most tender feelings and kindnesses to someone for his or her enjoyment. And you know what you're doing by railing on Brad expresses a part of who you are but not the deepest part. You know it's wrong, and you want to do better."[2]

And then an affirming exposure of the spiritual dynamics at work in her soul, the realities placed in her heart by God's Spirit, might follow. "When Brad picks on you, you're vaguely aware that there is something about you he cannot destroy, a solidness, a wholeness that could free you to stand calmly in the face of his assaults, hurting but not devastated, disappointed, even angry, but not murderous. We could trace all the harshness and abuse you've ever faced and find an identity that has survived, intact, maybe beaten, but still alive."

Finally the good urges toward Brad could be exposed. "The gospel frees you to do whatever you most truly want to do as you enjoy the embrace of your Father. Share with Brad what comes out of you as you remain still in the arms of God."

The last thought needs clarification. Her deepest, Spirit-led impulse may be to strongly rebuke Brad, to remove herself from the range of his abuse if that abuse is severe. But the passions that flow from her new heart will be tender, redemptive, unthreatened, firm but kind.

Part of the power of looking for the good beneath the bad comes from the agenda we often have when we let others see our ugliness. There may be a test: "Will you see no more than my ugliness? If so, then I'll feel justified in looking out for myself, whatever further ugliness that may require."

We become hardened when people react to our ugliness with inquisitiveness or rebuke. But when a friend meets our meanness with kindness, something better often comes out of us.

Or, we may intensify the test. "I *must* know you believe in me. I'll let you see so much bad stuff that if you continue to calmly search for the good, then maybe I'll be able to believe that something good might actually be there."

The second element is a diligent search for what is good.

ELEMENT #3.

AN ENGAGING EXPOSURE OF WHAT IS BAD OR PAINFUL

Notice this element comes last. Too often we put it first. I am persuaded that if we provide others with a delightful taste of Christ and if we eagerly search for the good going on in their hearts, this final ingredient will become less frequently necessary.

There are times, however, when goodness is most fully released only when badness is first resisted. That resistance may require the special encouragement of seeing grace at work when judgment is most deserved. Connecting helps not only to enliven the good but also to destroy the bad, and it does so by surprising us with forgiving love.

By our sin, we have created our state of disconnection from God, ourselves, and others.

Out of his great love, God has taken it upon himself to reconnect us, first to himself by revealing that he is *that* good; then to ourselves and others by pouring his goodness into our hearts, a goodness that enables us to live with integrity, prompted by spiritual dynamics, and aware of urges within us to bless others.

Sometimes he furthers the process of reconnecting by exposing our bad inclinations to make it on our own resources, deny our longings, lower our moral standards, preserve ourselves in the face of danger, and use others to our advantage. When he exposes the badness and pain and tension within us, we are disrupted. It throws us off balance, sometimes severely.

An earlier book of mine, *Inside Out*, offered a guided tour of our internal world. That tour revealed that we are always aching for something better and reliably sinning in our efforts to keep ourselves alive. Many have told me that they couldn't read that book without hurling it several times across the room. Exposure of pain and sin is difficult.

But God's message throughout the exposure process is not "You're *that* bad, and don't you forget it!" or "Your pain is so extreme you must trust or be destroyed!" but rather "I'm *that* good. I still like you. I'm for you. I want you to know it. And what's ahead for you is beyond description."

When badness is exposed for the purpose of more fully revealing the depths of God's kindness and his promise of fun forever, then disruption is productive. A simple example will make the point. Too often, parents spank their children in anger. That never helps. Angry efforts to control a son or daughter never release good things in the child. But when a parent disciplines a child out of loving hope for what the child could become, when the intent is to restore and develop, not punish and control, then the disruption that discipline brings can promote good results.

It requires less formal training and more self-awareness to know what to expose, to recognize what is bad within ourselves and others. An honest look at ourselves will reveal our suspicion that God isn't good enough (otherwise *this* would never have happened); our refusal to embrace how deeply disappointed and alone we sometimes feel; our habit of reducing moral standards to levels that help us feel good about ourselves; the thousand ways we receive the harsh impact of our world and quickly react to preserve our sense of a worthy self (a choice that Jesus told us will erode our sense of personal identity); and our self-centered maneuverings in relationships that we pass off as noble or at least justified.

If we see ourselves clearly, we will be able to see into the tangled heart of another (Matt. 7:3–5). But when we do, we must make it our goal to reconnect people with the heart of God through our exposure of their darkness.

That's what God does. He exposes the bad to reveal the good.[3] That's what we therefore must do as well.

Listen to what we might hear our Lord say to a husband who has demeaned his wife.

> Yes, you just sniped at your wife. It was unjustified, cruel, and harmful. But you must not focus on why you did it. You already know that in your flesh you're selfish, insecure, demanding, and petty.
>
> I want you to notice, however, that you're bothered by it. You're inclined to stifle the voice of conscience and justify your meanness, to pretend it doesn't matter that you and your wife are a million emotional miles apart.
>
> But you're also inclined to feel your sadness and acknowledge your wrong. That's the beginning of brokenness.
>
> And you want to do better. There's a bit a repentance. Something quietly stirring in you wants to make amends, to forgive her for her failures and to beg her forgiveness. Good! That's the inclination of your new heart.
>
> Let me strengthen that urge. It will grow and be released as you experience how I feel about you right now as you stand there exposed as a mean-spirited, arrogant man. You're forgiven, the fatted calf is prepared and ready to roast on the fire, the angelic choir is in dress rehearsal. I can see the glory in you right now. You want to love her well. I'm jumping up and down with excitement. You want to love like me. The appetite is there.
>
> And when you experience how I'm looking at you as you stand there naked and ashamed, you'll move toward your wife differently. I'm too good to resist. Taste and see!

Relationships heal when they reflect the energy of Christ. We can impact others by:

- letting people know we delight in them as Christ does;

- eagerly looking for the goodness in someone's heart and identifying the passions that are prompting loving, strong choices;

- exposing the darkness in someone's heart, their sin and pain, in order to engage them more convincingly with the Savior's kindness; it's the kindness of God that leads to repentance.

These three ingredients of powerfully healing relationships are available to every Christian but practiced so little. However, when they are practiced, even when only the first ingredient is in place, enormous good can result. Read on.

CHAPTER 3

Restored through Reconnecting

W hen *things change for the better,* we usually feel better. But for spiritual writer Henri Nouwen, when relocation to a new ministry provided him with richer community, he experienced the darkest night of his soul.

Listen to his words:

> After many years of life in universities, where I never felt fully at home, I had become a member of L'Arche, a community of men and women with disabilities. I had been received with open arms, given all the attention and affection I could ever hope for, and offered a safe and loving place to grow spiritually as well as emotionally. Everything seemed ideal. But precisely at that time I fell apart—as if I needed a safe place to hit bottom.[1]

As soon as I read those words, my psychologist mind went to work. Why would a new atmosphere of safety trigger Nouwen's sudden descent into despair? Were there buried longings that had never surfaced before, intense longings that were perhaps left over from unresolved difficulties in earlier years? For a long time, Nouwen had enjoyed enough props to support anyone's self-esteem: successful academic life at a prestigious university, well-received books, wide recognition as a serious reflective thinker.

When he gave them up for life with people who were not impressed by such things, perhaps his repressed desire to be loved rather than merely admired overwhelmed him. The taste of love that his new community provided may have awakened deeper longings than he ever knew existed, longings that he feared would never be satisfied.

And then, in the middle of my analytic fantasy, I thought how powerless I would feel sharing all this with Nouwen. I'm sure he would have listened attentively, but my analysis would not, I fear, have helped him. I realized that, *as a psychologist,* I felt abysmally inadequate to help.

I tried to picture myself as Nouwen's therapist, treating the psychological disorder that most mental health professionals would assume lay beneath his distressing symptoms. And I felt not only powerless but also silly. This profound man's struggles could not be contained by the usual categories of explanation. My imagined efforts to "treat" a psychological disorder seemed to cheapen the mysterious battle raging deep in his soul. To reduce that battle to my neat little packages felt wrong.

I was struck by how inclined I am to cram people's lives into boxes that I can understand and so feel better about myself. Someone said that if the only tool you have is a hammer, everything looks like a nail. If my best efforts to help fall under the category of therapy, then I will want to see the problem I'm trying to treat as evidence of psychological pathology.

I sometimes think five years of graduate school trained me to shrink the questions people ask down to a size I can handle. But Nouwen makes that difficult. He described his battle in hard-to-shrink language. Listen again.

> That was a time of extreme anguish, during which I wondered whether I would be able to hold on to my own life. Everything came crashing down—my self-esteem, my energy to love and work, my sense of being loved, my hope for healing, my trust in God . . . everything. Here I was, a writer about the spiritual life, known as someone who loves God and gives hope to people, flat on the ground and in total darkness.
>
> I experienced myself as a useless, unloved, and despicable person. Just when people were putting their arms around me, I saw the endless depth of my human misery and felt that there was nothing worth living for. All had become darkness. Within me there was one

long scream coming from a place I didn't know existed, a place full of demons.[2]

What do we do with such a man? We immediately feel powerless, the way we feel when *anyone* lets us into the darkest rooms—or even just the foyer—of their innermost being. Not many could describe it as eloquently as Nouwen, but most of us know what it is to look in the mirror and see someone despicable, to listen to the deep places we try to pretend aren't there and hear one long scream of despair.

I recently sat with a friend over lunch. The conversation turned weighty. I chose to share that I was living in a tunnel of discouragement so dark that I had no energy left to keep moving. I could feel his immediate discomfort. He didn't know what to say.

I don't blame him. I'm not sure what I wanted him to say. Should he probe? Should he invite specific disclosure of things in my life that I am finding troublesome? Would it be better to quietly listen to whatever more I wanted to share? Should he pray? Should he recommend I schedule time with my pastor or a counselor?

When people make their struggles known, those who listen usually feel uncomfortable and uncertain of what to do. Most of us end up giving advice or reassurance that draws a courteous yawn. We rarely see such moments as opportunity for powerful connection, or, if we do, we're not sure how to seize it.

The moralists among us may not feel so inadequate. Like an impatient farmer commanding an apple tree to bear fruit in winter, a moralist might come up with a list of good things for someone like Nouwen to do, things that depressed people often let slide—getting up early for devotions, encouraging others, doing the laundry, eating properly.

The usual pattern for most of us in dealing with a hurting friend is to *retreat, reprove,* or *refer.* Like Israelites avoiding a leper, most of us want to establish a safe distance between us and the emotionally troubled. We often do so by reciting Christian phrases that arouse no passion in us but are supposed to do powerful things for them. "God is at work even in the darkest of times" or "Where has the Word ministered to you recently?" or "You really have no reason to be so down. You're too hard on yourself.

You have a lot going for you." The effect is to free us from such confusing conversations with "sick" people so that we can move on to hang around happier folks.

Or we try to scold people into holier living. Reproving another provides an easy route to representing God without the hard work of involvement. It's Sinai without Bethlehem; legislation without incarnation; only Moses, never Christ.

Perhaps the most popular reaction when we encounter a struggling person is to refer: "I wonder if you should be talking to someone about this. Have you considered counseling?"

Suppose a friend had referred Nouwen to a typical therapist. Most therapists, if only for insurance purposes, consult the *Diagnostic and Statistical Manual of Mental Disorders*. In the Fourth Edition, on page 320, in the section titled "Mood Disorder," we're told that "The essential feature of a Major Depressive Episode is a period of at least two weeks during which there is either a depressed mood or the loss of interest or pleasure in nearly all activities."

The assumption, of course, is that certain symptoms, as in medicine, point to an underlying disorder, a *mental* or *emotional* illness that requires professional treatment.

Nouwen reported that he ". . . no longer had any interest in other people's problems. I lost all appetite for food and could not appreciate the beauty of music, art, or even nature."[3] His dark mood and inability to feel pleasure lasted several months. Combined with a variety of other symptoms, these problems would likely justify a diagnosis of Major Depressive Disorder, Single Episode, Severe, Without Psychotic Features: Code #296.23. Even the habit of capitalizing the words that make up the diagnosis encourages the notion that we are dealing with a disorder in need of treatment.

The message is clear: *The power to help a diagnosed patient depends on proper training.* Only a professional psychotherapist is equipped to handle problems such as those Nouwen reported.

But suppose we're wrong. Suppose that many of the struggles we assume are symptoms of a psychological disorder are in fact evidence of a disconnected soul. If the core problem beneath Nouwen's "depression" or your daughter's fanatic commitment to thinness or your husband's workaholism or your friend's obsession with pornography or your own inability to get close to anybody is an empty soul, a soul starving for life, then connecting with a source of life, not professional treatment, is called for. But we're not sure what it means to connect with someone so richly that life goes out of one and into another.

In a different place, Nouwen tells us one thing he did during his season of anguish. With deep appreciation, he speaks of an elderly friend, a priest, to whom he turned.

> During the most difficult period of my life, when I experienced great anguish and despair, he was there. Many times, he pulled my head to his chest and prayed for me without words but with a Spirit-filled silence that dispelled my demons of despair and made me rise up from his embrace with new vitality.[4]

"He pulled my head to his chest." The result was that Nouwen rose up "with new vitality." Is that what I did with my son Kep when he got in trouble? Could I do it with others? Is that what good therapists and shepherds do? Could I do it as a lifestyle? Could everyone connect like that with a few others?

Two sets of questions lunge at me as I read this unusual account of healing. *First, do I want someone to pull my head to his or her chest?* It sounds so needy, so weak, almost pathetic. A toddler bumps into a table and cries. Seasoned mothers know the tears express a desire to be held; they're more than a demand for relief from the actual pain. The kiss that makes it better has no anesthetic quality. The pain remains, but the child's soul is soothed by connecting with the mother. When mother pulls the child's head to her chest, something happens that makes the pain seem less important.

But I'm an adult, not a child. Being a patient to a therapist seems more dignified than being a frightened little lamb held in the strong arms of a shepherd. To let someone hold me requires that I admit how badly I want it, how much I long to connect with someone powerful and good. And that offends my pride.

And it also leaves me confused. Do I need to be held? Will connecting heal whatever lies at the root of psychological disorder? Can words embrace the soul as arms embrace the body?

I wonder if we *like* to think of our problems as evidence of psychological disorder because we lack the courage to be broken by our loneliness and need. Perhaps that same lack of courage fuels the moralist's determination to fit every problem into the box of undisciplined living and unconfessed sin.

As I read of an older man pulling Nouwen's head to his chest, I cannot deny how badly I want someone to do that for me. But as soon as that longing is aroused, I feel fear: fear that I'm an insecure, neurotic baby for wanting it; fear that you'll think I'm an insecure, neurotic baby for wanting it; fear that no one will let me be that weak without scorning me; fear that if I'm held, I'll never get up and move with strength again.

I want someone to pull my head to his or her chest. But I also want to pull someone's head to mine. I want to be both dependent and powerful. Is the dependency legitimate? Is it evidence of design or weakness? Can I be powerful without first experiencing my dependency?

That leads me to the *second* set of questions: *What does it take to be powerful?* What kind of person can hold someone, silently pray, and in the process actually nourish a human soul with a renewed experience of life? What does it take? Training? Degrees? Licenses? Or is something else required?

When folks have prayed for me, I've often (not always) felt bored. I wonder how many I've bored with my powerless prayers. And I wonder how many of my therapy patients experienced more *intensity* in our sessions than *power*, more dramatic excitement over new ideas and feelings than deep lasting change.

The fact is that not many people powerfully connect with others, whether through prayer, embrace, or conversation. Connection could be the norm—instead it's the exception. Most people never even get a taste.

But kids could feel it through their parents. Our mates and friends could experience it through us. When connection occurs, it changes our lives. What's required to make it happen? And what is it about connecting that does the healing? What *is* connection? What came out of me with the power to touch Kep's heart and awaken his longing to connect with God?

We must find the courage to face our terrifying longing to connect, to accept another pulling our head to his or her chest, and to trust that strength will be provided to get up and leave that connecting embrace with renewed life; or, if no embrace comes, to go on with desperate dependence on God.

The story of Henri Nouwen's struggle leaves me with these two questions:

1. *Is the terrifying longing for connection evidence of weakness or design?* Should I honor the longing even though it scares me to death, or is it better to suppress it and get on with my life? Am I really that needy?

2. *What does it take to be a powerful person,* someone who connects so deeply with another that power comes out of my being that enables the other to rise up with a new sense of vitality—and maybe with a "cure" for whatever psychological disorder was thought to be present? Can we all become powerful enough to stir up life in one or two others?

The next several chapters deal with these questions.

CHAPTER 4

Designed to Connect

Ordinary people have the power to change other people's lives. An older priest can revitalize a despairing younger colleague by pulling the troubled man's head to his chest. A distraught father can touch his son with an energy that cuts through a hardened heart and awakens what is tender and true within the child. An adult daughter can offer something from hidden places within her to her aging mother that releases hope in the elderly woman's heart, hope that can support her through her loneliness, confusion, and pain.

The power is found in connection, that profound meeting when the truest part of one soul meets the emptiest recesses in another and finds something there, when life passes from one to the other. When that happens, the giver is left more full than before and the receiver less terrified, eventually eager, to experience even deeper, more mutual connection. The power to meaningfully change lives depends not on advice, though counsel and rebuke play a part; not on insight, though self-awareness that disrupts complacency and points toward new understanding is important; but on connecting, on bringing two people into an experience of shared life.

When our younger son Ken was eight years old, he loved to jump in puddles left by heavy Florida afternoon rains. After one particularly generous downpour, I grabbed our raincoats and boots and said, "Let's go!" When we returned an hour later, soaked and happy, Ken exclaimed, "Dad, that was fun. *I didn't know you were going to jump in the puddles*

31

too!" There's something about togetherness, at any level, that affects the heart.

I have come to believe that the root of all our personal and emotional difficulties is a lack of togetherness, a failure to connect that keeps us from receiving life and prevents the life in us from spilling over onto others. I therefore believe that the surest route to overcoming problems and becoming the people we were meant to be is reconnecting with God and with our community. But reconnecting, at its most healing levels, is no simple matter. In our fast-paced, get-it-done culture, it is rare. What we often call connecting is no more meaningful than a flight attendant's "Good to have you on board" recited to every departing passenger. Eyes meet, quick smiles are exchanged, a moment of warmth is felt—and the meeting is over, instantly forgotten, with no lingering effect.

Reconnecting a detached soul to the lifeblood of community requires power that only a few people seem to possess. Powerful people can see the hidden life that is already poured into another by God and, with an awareness of the life they have received from the same source, they pour out what is deepest and truest and noblest within them into the soul of another; and they do it with a clear vision of what that other person could become as the life of Christ is nourished and released within.

Powerful people believe in what others could become because they believe the good that exists deep within every regenerate heart is potentially stronger than all the bad that is there. Powerful people accept the challenge to identify, nourish, and release the life of God in others by connecting with them.

Exhorting a son to be moral has its place. Exposing the insecurities that might make temptation even more attractive may help. But without loving connection, neither has power. Without awakening the *urge* to be moral, the best one can hope for is rigid conformity (the fruit of moralism) or adaptive conformity (the fruit of therapy). Without connection, glad obedience flowing out of a changed heart is not an option.

But that's not how most people in our culture think. When we see a problem in ourselves or others, our minds typically move in one of two directions: Either we assume a *stubborn will* is behind the difficulty ("That kid just won't cooperate with our family's standards!") or we wonder if something is *psychologically wrong* ("Maybe he has low self-esteem. When I was starting my business, I didn't spend much time with him. I'll bet he felt abandoned and angry.")

Those who see stubbornness as the root cause behind people's problems try to promote change according to something we might call the *exhortation/accountability* model. According to this thinking, efforts to help consist largely of admonishment to do what's right, with painful consequences for violation and, occasionally, rewards for cooperation. The power we depend on to influence someone's life then becomes pressure in all its ugly forms: guilt, shame, threat, fear, manipulation, to name a few.

Admonishment to do right becomes ugly pressure when it is not preceded and liberally accompanied by an attitude that says, "I cannot make you do anything. But I believe there is something in you that knows what you're doing is wrong and, if you belong to God, there is something in you that wants to do right. I believe in that life within you. I trust God's work in you. And more than anything else, I want you to enjoy a taste of God's gracious, loving heart in your relationship with me."

When would-be helpers define other people as little more than choosing beings and treat them as bad decision makers who must be instructed and held accountable in good decisions, their efforts to help are only an investigation of what someone is doing wrong and an exhortation to do something right. Parental scoldings, pastoral rebukes, church and family discipline, and group accountability often fall into this category with predictable results—sometimes conformity, often rebellion, never maturity.

Not everyone, of course, accepts this model of change. The scores of people influenced by our therapeutic culture have been taught to think differently. They are careful to understand, never blame. For them, moral judgment causes problems; it doesn't solve them. A problem—whether anxiety, overeating, or addictions—signals the presence of a deeper problem within. Moralistic entreaty is worse than useless because the cause beneath the difficulty is not stubbornness. It is emotional damage or psychological disorder. Advice is impotent. Rebuke is harmful.

The *treatment/repair* model is quickly called in: We must find a way to fix what's wrong. The first step, of course, is to figure out what is wrong (diagnosis) and face it, then courageously work through the often long and painful process of coming to grips with the internal damage and learning to approach life in healthier ways (therapy). In this model hurting people are thought of as psychological beings, a viewpoint that recognizes their ability to choose but highlights the deep, often unconscious, forces within them that influences their choices. I recently spoke with a divorced mother about her troublesome son. "He comes home from school in a bad mood and goes straight to his room. If I try to engage him in conversation, he either grunts something or is positively rude. I can't tell his father what he's like because he thinks I just need to be firmer; and then when he gets our son on weekends, he comes down really hard on him. And that makes matters worse. I think my son is really struggling with something. I've wondered if he blames himself for his dad leaving. All his anger toward me may be his way of coping with self-hatred."

In this view, the power to change depends on insight, not pressure; self-awareness, not rules; psychological understanding, not commands. Communities that heal are communities that probe and expose, that help people to see what's going on inside them and encourage them to handle their struggles more effectively.

And changes do occur. But without connection, without the life of Christ being aroused by a stronger measure of that life being poured out from another, increased self-awareness at best leads to more sociable and adaptive patterns of selfishness.

Let me reduce to a sketch what I've just explained.

If people at core are stubborn, if we exercise our wills in bad directions when we could exercise them to move in good ones, and if our bad choices are the root cause of what is wrong, then scoldings are called for. And they must have teeth. Much of what we call Christian counseling, especially in more "biblical" circles, is little more than the application of the law to life. Do you have a problem? Find someone who knows the Bible well enough to tell you what principle needs to be more carefully observed and what actions are required to put it into practice.

If, however, people at core are more damaged than stubborn, if our sense of self is fragile or perverted or underdeveloped, then an exploration of that damage seems appropriate. Freud's original idea was to bring unconscious forces into the light where they would no longer

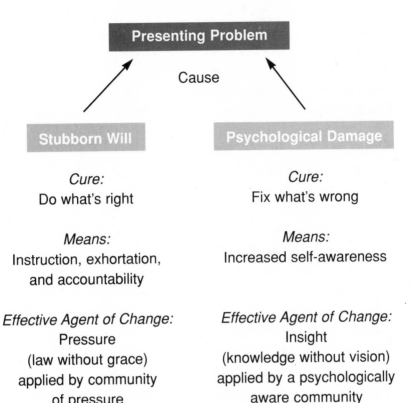

compulsively control us, where we could see them as irrational and no longer automatically yield to them.

Neither approach gets at the center of who we are as image-bearing creatures of a trinitarian God. We are, of course, both stubborn and blind. The law does expose our stubbornness for what it is, and honest examination of our hearts and our histories will often surface a complex of psychological "stuff" that might never otherwise be acknowledged.

But, although we are both stubborn and damaged, fundamentally we are neither. At the exact center of the human personality is a capacity to give and receive in relationship, a capacity or possibility that defines what it means to be alive as a human being. When that capacity is corrupted, when, rather than giving who we are and receiving others for who they are, we use others to gain what we think we need and to protect ourselves from the harm others can inflict on us, then we are dead. We are sub-human. We give evidence that we have fallen to a level lower than our intended humanity.

When God forgives us for violating his design, he pours his life into us; and that restores our capacity to connect, first with him, then with others. He makes us alive with the actual life of Christ. The energy with which Jesus heard and obeyed the Father, the impulses that lay behind every-thing he did—his tenderness with the lame man, his indignation with the moneychangers, his patience with Philip, his red-hot scorn of the Pharisees, his love for children, his resolve to endure injustice without complaint—are in us. *The impulses that energized Jesus' life on earth are actually in us.* That's part of what it means to be alive in Christ.

Non-Christians do not have that life. They are still dead in sin, separate from God, controlled by a very different energy. Non-Christians are com-mitted to using resources under their control to make life work for them and to experience whatever satisfying quality of life they can arrange. They do not have the life of Christ as an available energy. Their energy consists of anti-God independence, self-reliance, a "get what you need for yourself then worry about someone else" attitude. That energy can be socialized, but it can never be changed. Selfishness can never be *improved into* some-thing good, but it can be *replaced by* something good.

At the core of non-Christians, however, is the same capacity for rela-tionship that exists at the core of Christians. Everyone was designed to connect. In non-Christians, though that capacity is functionally dead, there is a haunting memory of what once was, a lingering appetite for what could be.

When a person possessing the life of Christ pours that life into non-Christians, the memory gets clearer, the appetite deepens. When the Spirit of God then whispers, "This is what you've been looking for," he draws non-Christians to Christ, to the source of the connection for which they long.

In Christ, people are then forgiven and quickened, adopted as mem-bers of the family of God and provided with the *nature* of that family. There is restored capacity to relate, complete with a brand-new set of inclinations to relate the way Christ relates.

But, unlike in Christ, those good urges compete with bad urges that remain within, bad urges that are no longer at the precise center but close enough to it to often feel as though they are. The task, beginning at conversion and lasting until heaven, is to identify, nourish, and release those good urges. We do that for each other by connecting.

We make a serious mistake when we substitute moralism for connection. When we think that pressuring people to do what's right will promote good change, we aren't concerned with connecting with people. We address the will and require its cooperation rather than connect with the heart to release the life of Christ that God has placed in its center.

One writer put it this way: The question is not how the Christian "can realize the good by his own power but how he is to realize himself by the power of the good . . . which is already there."[1] When the Christian community seeks to change people merely by getting them to do the right thing, it loses its power. When efforts to counsel biblically are reduced to exposing wrong and exhorting right, our "life in Christ" is smothered.

We make a second mistake, equally serious, when we abandon pressure and embrace insight as the route to change. When we regard a deeper awareness of all that is going on inside us as the power that will change lives, we end up exploring our internal mess so thoroughly that we never find our true identity.

I remember speaking with a woman struggling with self-hatred. She criticized herself for every mistake she made, relentlessly, mercilessly. Months of therapy had uncovered a traumatic past, complete with abuse, rejection, and neglect. The assumption shared by both therapist and patient was that these experiences had wrongly taught her to hate herself as her only means of survival, something like hitting yourself before someone else does. If you're already lying on the ground, you might be less likely to suffer another blow.

She reported all this with what felt to me like morbid excitement. And then she said, "My therapist senses that my hand is on the knob of a door leading to another dark room and that I must find the courage to turn it and walk in. He thinks there is more abuse I haven't yet faced."

But suppose there is a room in her soul that is full of light. Must she explore every dark room before finding and entering it? Will she find "herself" by stumbling into every musty, forbidding closet? Or is her true self existing already in a wonderfully bright, lavishly furnished room that sits in the very center of her house, a *living* room, a room she has never entered?

Jesus made it clear that a search for ourselves in all that is natural to us will always prove disappointing. "Simon the fisherman could have explored every region of his ego prior to his encounter with Christ but he would not have found 'Peter' there." The true identity of Peter, the man created to replace Simon, was "hidden in the mystery of Christ's soul." [2]

We will not heal many souls when advice or instruction is at the center of our efforts. Our power to influence lives does not come from telling people what to do.

Nor does it come from revealing to people the details of their internal mess.

Healing community does not depend on getting people to do what's right or on figuring out what harmful psychological forces are causing us problems and then trying to fix what's wrong. A community that heals is a community that believes the gospel provides *forgiveness* of all sin, a guaranteed *future* of perfect community forever, and the *freedom* now to indulge the deepest desires of our hearts, because the law of God is written within us—we have an appetite for holiness. Communities heal when they focus on releasing what's good.

Our sketch can now be completed.

Let me put it plainly. The center of a forgiven person is not sin. Neither is it psychological complexity. The center of a person is the capacity to connect.

Either we can live as unique members of a connected community, experiencing the fruit of Christ's life within us, or we can live as terrified, demanding, self-absorbed islands, disconnected from community and desperately determined to get by with whatever resources we brought to our island with us.

The calling of community is to lure people off the island onto the mainland where connection is possible and to provide it. Only then do we truly bear the image of the Eternal Community who created us to enjoy connecting.

Presenting Problem

Cause

Stubborn Will

Cure:
Do what's right

Means:
Instruction, exhortation,
and accountability

Effective Agent of Change:
Pressure
(law without grace)
applied by community
of pressure

Psychological Damage

Cure:
Fix what's wrong

Means:
Increased self-awareness

Effective Agent of Change:
Insight
(knowledge without vision)
applied by a psychologically
aware community

Disconnected Soul

Cure:
Release what's good

Means:
Identify and nourish new life

Effective Agent of Change:
Connecting
(pouring life into another)
applied through a community
of a connected few

Connected community, not good advice, not deeper insight, is at the center of things. Why? *Because connected community is the defining center of God.* When we grasp that truth, we will embark on the journey toward connection. That's my next topic.

CHAPTER 5

Connecting: The Center of Life

*C*huck *approached me during* a week-long conference and said, "Larry, Dick and Don and a few other of your friends would like to take you out for breakfast tomorrow morning. Would that work?"

With the innocence of a trusting child, I assumed that my good friends wanted simply to enjoy my company over eggs and pancakes. Six of us piled into one car early the next morning. During the ten-minute drive we laughed, bantered pleasantly, and shared some good-natured ribbing.

At the restaurant the mood changed. As soon as the food arrived, Chuck, a deeply respected friend with a gentle spirit and a heart committed to my welfare, cleared his throat and began.

"Larry, we got to thinking among ourselves what it's like to have you for a friend. We were talking about you behind your back, and we thought it would be better to tell you directly about our conversation."

Nearly everything in me wanted to suggest there was no need to let me in on their thoughts—I sensed they were not preparing to pass along compliments—but a deeper part within me trusted these men. I knew they accepted me. Whatever they might say, I reminded myself, would grow out of a vision they had for the man I could become. I struggled to listen.

The next ninety minutes of input can be summarized in a few sentences: "You give us more of your head than your heart. When we share a personal burden with you, you immediately go to work. You give us great counsel and perceptive insights, but we want more of you. We know it's there, and we think it would do more for us to feel your heart than all your wise words."

The Bible states that "wounds from a friend can be trusted" (Prov. 27:6). I pondered what I had heard. I became aware of how desperately I work to lead with what I assumed to be my strength. And I realized, with fresh clarity, how terrified I am to simply *be* in someone else's presence. There's no power to my being. It's my training, my giftedness, my experience that makes a difference. And besides, if you reject my wisdom, I can study more, read more, think more. But if you reject *me,* there's no place to hide.

It was shortly after that encounter that an acquaintance of mine tried to commit suicide. What he did should have killed him, but he survived. I was asked to help. For more than six months I worked with this man in therapy. Even now I recall the session—I think it was the tenth—where I came up with an insight that put so much of his pain into new perspective. I remember him saying, "How on earth did you figure that out?" I humbly shrugged and said, "Hope it helps."

In the middle of our work together, I happened one spring day to be driving through the local college campus and saw my depressed client sitting on the grass with a friend. They were laughing. I'm not clear why, but I felt a strong desire to join their good time.

Every reason why I shouldn't join them ran instantly through my head—too much to do, it would be awkward, even unprofessional, to socialize with a client—but the words of my friends over breakfast came back to me. Was I afraid to just *be* with this man, to take off the Dr. Crabb white coat, to stop being an expert, and offer myself as a person?

On an impulse, I stopped my car, walked over to where they were sitting, their backs toward me. When I got close, they heard my footsteps, and turned. I greeted them both, then said to my client, "How are you?"

Picture what it would be like to have your therapist, while you're in the middle of treatment for suicidal depression, walk up to you in a casual setting and ask, "How are you?"

He wrinkled his face into a serious expression, coughed a few times, then said, "Well, maybe a little better. Still really worried about . . ."

I interrupted. "I don't mean, 'How are you doing with your struggles?' I'm just sociably asking how you're doing."

He replied, "You mean like, 'Fine, thanks'?"

"Yes, exactly!"

"In that case, fine, thanks. Can you join us?"

"Sure, I've got some time."

For the next thirty minutes I didn't say one intelligent thing. I just enjoyed two friends.

Three years later I met him for coffee during a trip to the town where he was then living. He was doing well. At one point in our conversation he thanked me for my influence on his life. I asked what he remembered that had helped the most. There was no hesitation.

"It was that half hour you sat on the grass with me and my friend and just chatted." He was warmly smiling.

I was indignant. "Don't you recall that life-changing insight I came up with in the tenth session of therapy?"

"Uh, no, I don't. Can you refresh me?"

I believe that the work we did in therapy was important. But I also believe that the time I most clearly led with my heart rather than my head was the time of greatest power. Perhaps then he could trust whatever else I said. Or perhaps that moment on the lawn did the most actual healing.

I am proposing a new center for our efforts to help people, a center that counselors can revolve their work around, a center for parents and spouses to honor in building strong families, a center that can become the hub of church life.

For too long, the moralists among us have placed good advice at the center. That puts pressure on listeners to figure out what people who share their problems ought to do. The therapeutically inclined place a high premium on psychological insight, on coming up with a clever understanding of what's happening inside a person that only highly trained professionals can manage.

For most ordinary Christians, the center of helping efforts is simple kindness, warm affirmation, and words of encouragement. When they don't do the job, we quickly suggest that help be sought from a pastor or counselor.

There is obviously a place for advice, insight, and friendly encouragement—but not at the center. I suggest that the absolute center of all powerful attempts to impact people for good is connecting.

Earlier, I offered a beginning definition of connecting as something that occurs when the life of Christ in one person is poured into another and awakens in the emptiest recesses of that other person's soul the experience of life.

I want to think more about what connecting is and why I believe it is at the center of powerful relationships.

If connecting is at the center of healing, then disconnecting must be at the core of what needs healing. In our therapeutic way of thinking, we're more inclined to regard emotional forces, often unconscious, as the culprit behind the problems we face. Psychological dynamics active deep within our personalities become the object of study, interpretation, and treatment.

But maybe our real problem has more to do with the absence or the quenching of *spiritual* dynamics. "The Greek word that is used most frequently with reference to the power of the Holy Spirit is *dunamis,* power."[1] The word means not only dynamite but also dynamic, that which is lively and active. When the Spirit of God is dynamic in our lives, his central job is connecting us with God, convincing us of our need for a Savior, drawing us to Christ, whispering to us that God is our father, making clear to us the truth of God from Scripture, coming alongside of us to console us when we're wounded, to equip and strengthen us for the work we're called to do, and to empower us to relate to others with the energy of Christ.

No problem is deeper or more significant than the absence or minimization of this connecting force. Christians have long believed that the central difficulty in human existence is separation from God (we're under his judgment), from ourselves (we can't face what's true about us, either the extent of our sin or the depth of our pain), and from others (we demand from others rather than give to them).

That separation is what I mean by disconnection. In less theological terms, disconnection can be regarded as a state of being, a condition of existence where *the deepest part of who we are is vibrantly attached to no one, where we are profoundly unknown and therefore experience neither the thrill of being believed in nor the joy of loving or being loved.* Disconnected people may often be unaware of the empty recesses in their souls that long to be filled. They often mistake lesser longings for greater ones and settle for the satisfaction of popularity, influence, success, and intense but shallow relationships. Disconnected people are unaware of what God has placed within them that if poured into others could change lives. They feel either inadequate for questionable reasons or powerful for wrong reasons.

One friend has been endowed with ample supplies of wit, intuition, and money. It has taken him years to realize that there is a deeper life within him that impacts people far more profoundly than his obvious resources. Like all of us, he is terrified to stop depending on available resources under his control and to present himself as a mere person. As a result, as long as that terror rules in his approach to relationship, he meets no one. He remains disconnected.

If you carefully look beneath all the nonphysiologically caused problems that therapists label as psychological disorders, you will find disconnected souls, people whose attempts to live life in their own strength have left them isolated, detached, and alone. If we focus our helping efforts on uncovering and resolving the unhealthy psychological forces operating within them, we miss the core problem. If we advise them to live more consistently with biblical principles without offering meaningful connection, we leave them frustrated.

If, as we work to expose the deeper sinful patterns of idolatry and self-centered demandingness in the hopes of calling forth repentance, we never provide a deep taste of connection, we distort conviction and repentance into mechanical processes that do not lead to reconnection. They lead, at best, to smug righteousness and the illusion of growth.

Connecting is not the only necessary ingredient in powerful relating, but it is central. It is the core good news of the gospel. Why? It's what we most want, what we most lack, what we most fear will never be ours.

The deepest urge in every human heart is to be in relationship with someone who absolutely delights in us, someone with resources we lack who has no greater joy than giving to us, someone who respects us enough to require us to use everything we receive for the good of others, and because he has given it to us, knows we have something to give. The longing to connect defines our dignity as human beings and our destiny as image-bearers.

Everyone shares the same longing, Christian or not. Christians too often bury their longings under a commitment to keep the rules. Secularists are sometimes more honest about their longings and better take them into account.

But secularists are wrong when they assert, as they commonly do, that connection is available through unconditional positive regard. They tell us that if we draw deeply from the depths of our own souls in order to experience with others whatever they feel and then grant them our thorough acceptance, we're connecting.

Carl Rogers, the major figure in the field of psychology who pioneered this line of thinking, is dangerously and heretically wrong. He offers acceptance without the atonement and understanding rather than forgiveness. In his thinking, there is nothing terrible in us that requires forgiveness. The problem is *merely* disconnection, a state of detachment that is the result not of rebellious independence from God but of unfortunate psychological development. The atonement is therefore irrelevant. Unconditional positive regard is the total answer.

That's what many secularists teach. With all my heart, I believe they are wrong. Why then do I feel so drawn to the kind of community that Rogers envisions, where acceptance supplants judgment, where we continue calling out the good in each other in spite of whatever ugliness we see? Why do I want to see some of Rogers's thinking rub off on pastors and on me?

Why do I strongly yearn for the kind of connection that so few churches offer, the kind I rarely give others, the kind that is more eager to listen than advise, to embrace than probe, and to pour what is in one into another regardless of cost?

Rogers sees no need for the atonement. In his mind, there is no sin to forgive. Christians believe that without the atonement there is no forgiveness, without forgiveness there is no connection, and without connection there is the loneliness of hell forever. But we must be equally quick to teach that with the atonement there is forgiveness, with forgiveness there is connection, and with connection there is the community of faith, a community destined to enter the bliss of perfect connection forever. The point of the whole plan is relationship, a connected community.

We can make a little headway in building that community now. If I have already been forgiven and therefore connected to a God whose Spirit pours life into me, then you pose no threat to my existence. You can reject me, hurt me, and make my life pretty miserable, but you cannot destroy me. Therefore I don't need to be so afraid of you that my fear controls how I treat you.

I don't need to keep up my guard. I can actually accept you as God for Christ's sake has already accepted me. When you offend me, I can nourish the spirit of forgiveness within me because it's there. I may have to look hard for it, but it's there. I've been forgiven, and I've been given the urge to forgive, the same urge that led to my being forgiven. I can pour into you the life that has been poured into me.

During one of our difficult moments years ago, I told my son Kep that he had the power to hurt me as few other people did, but he did not have the power to destroy me; I could therefore keep loving him even when it felt that my survival seemed to depend on loving him less.

When we pour into another even a little of the life that, at the cost of Jesus' death, has been poured into us, connection happens. Reconnection takes place. A disconnected soul begins to draw closer, to discover the life that is already there but has never perhaps been richly experienced.

We realize that someone sees us as we are and still delights in us, still believes that we could become responsible, giving people, that someone sees us as *fundamentally acceptable.* Courage develops, hope appears, and we press on with life, eager not only to receive more connection but also to provide it for others.

Is there really a way for ordinary people, untrained in the theory and skills of counseling, to relate to others with a power that could change their lives? Could there really be "gospel communities"—in our homes, in our circle of friends, and in our churches—where soul care actually happens? Do we have a power within us waiting to be released that can draw sullen teenagers out of their funk into the joys of responsible living, restore self-control to men and women who can't seem to resist temptation, and give hope to discouraged and lonely people that their hearts could be full?

Can the parents of an overweight ten-year-old girl who every day at school hears boys call her "Fatty" speak powerfully into their daughter's life? If so, why do their efforts to comfort her often seem so anemic?

I was recently asked to speak to a young woman who two weeks earlier had accidentally backed her car over her seventeen-month-old daughter and killed her. Can anything be said that has even the vaguest hope of beginning the long process of healing?

What are grandparents to do when they observe their son-in-law control their grandchildren's lives with tyrantlike strictness? Should they speak up? If so, how? With cautious suggestions or straightforward candor? Or will any comment be heard as interference and just make matters worse for the grandkids? Maybe they should say nothing and pray like mad. Or perhaps they could offer to keep the grandkids for eight months every year.

When worried parents, guilt-ridden mothers, or concerned grandparents ask for help, what should a helper—whether pastor, counselor, or friend—do? It's always appropriate, of course, to listen well, relate empathically, and offer heartfelt and prayerful support. But so often that seems like telling a hungry person that you care without offering food. It simply isn't enough.

Critics of counseling are fond of saying, "All most people need is someone to listen to them." There's some truth to that. But the parents of the overweight girl want more than a friend who cares. And they want more than a friend who prays. They want to know how they can relate to their daughter in ways that will powerfully touch her wounded soul. In speaking with them, I want to be more than an affirming friend who assures them that they are good and decent parents. I also want to do more than try to figure out what biblical principles fit their situation and what they could be doing differently.

I want to be cautious about exploring whether they are disappointed or disgusted with their daughter's appearance. Looking for damaging attitudes in the parents, whether in hopes of curing those attitudes by understanding their unconscious roots or promoting repentance through brokenness over sin, is dangerous business. It can easily lead to an unhealthy focus on understanding and repairing internal problems that tries to attain good goals by a deeper psychological form of human effort (see Gal. 3:1–3).

There is, of course, a legitimate place for applying biblical principles and exploring things inside of us that we tend to deny. But when applying biblical principles *becomes the center* of our efforts to help, we become moralists. Our power reduces to pressure. And when probing into denied internal reality is *at the core* of our helping efforts, we join the therapeutic culture that emphasizes increased self-awareness as the key to change.

I am proposing a different center for powerful relating. Good friends hope that kind support will heal. I suggest connecting, a kind of relating that goes far beyond affirming and encouraging, is needed. Moralists think obedience should be the focus. I suggest that a heart inclined toward obedience is more the point. Therapists too often search for personal pathology the way physicians look for physical disease and then try to restore health. I recommend that we probe to discover what God is up to and join him in nourishing the life he has already given. It may be necessary to face what's wrong, not to make the wrong better, but to cut through it to find what's right.

When you see me struggling, realize that my worst fear is that I'm *nothing more* than a struggler, that nobody can see anything deeper in me than my sin and pain because that's all there is, that my only hope is to sin less and to somehow feel better. Don't put yourself under the pressure to figure out what I should do. That will confirm that my only hope is to do more right things. I've tried that. It doesn't work.

Don't play amateur therapist or quickly send me to a real one. You'll just intensify my search to find out what's wrong with me, and I'll likely become more self-preoccupied and Spirit quenching than ever. And don't merely be nice and promise to pray for me. You can do more than hug me and go through the motions of pulling my head to your chest.

When you see me filled with doubt and self-hatred, when you observe me during my worst seasons of discouragement and failure, I want you to be filled with both *anguish* (weep with me as I weep) and *hope,* not the empty hope that says trite things like "It'll all work out" or "Just hang in there—I'm sure you'll feel better soon," but a hope that exists because it sees something in me that is absolutely terrific. Believe that there is *life* in me. I want to catch the gleam in your eye that tells me you know there is more to me than my problems and that you're confidently hopeful that the good will emerge. I want you to ache when you see the good buried beneath so much bad, but I want you to be passionately convinced that, by the grace of God, the good is there waiting to be released.

Don't be intrusive. Build a bridge of trust before you pass weighty things out of your heart into mine. Chuck knew me well. He was my mentor. I wanted his input. The bridge was there. Let your bridge be the connection that pours the life of acceptance into my weary, thirsty soul.

If you believe that the gospel has given life to both of us, then you could learn to release the power of that life within you to nourish the life of goodness within me. And as you do that, the healing process begins, the center of soul care falls into place and you release the spiritual dynamic of powerful relating.

At this point, two questions press for a response. First, is connecting really that central? If so, why? Second, what is the good in Christians that makes connecting possible? Aren't we totally depraved with nothing good to offer?

The next several chapters respond to those questions.

CHAPTER 6

Connection and Vision

nswers to truly important questions are usually simple. But simple answers sometimes sound simplistic, like ideas that occur to us when we're too tired to think or the sweet mutterings of a kind old man who assures us that all the young rascals will turn out fine if we just believe in them.

People who love complexity because it provides an opportunity to parade their intellect are the least likely to appreciate simple answers. Their enjoyment of pursuing truth more than finding it disposes them to see simplicity as simplistic and confusion as profound.

There are, of course, simpletons, people who are drawn to superficial understandings because they're afraid, for whatever reason, of probing too deeply into the mysteries of life. These are the folks who give simplicity a bad name.

But simple answers that emerge out of a hard look into difficult matters are worth considering.

In this chapter, I propose the beginnings of a simple answer to an important question. Then I discuss a difficult matter that forms the basis of my simple answer. The important question is this: Is connecting really that central? If so, what's so powerful about it?

My simple answer is: Connecting is the center of everything, and a vision for what we could become gives it power. The difficult subject from which my simple answer comes is the *Trinity*.

The idea behind this book is that neither pleasant relating, moralistic relating, or therapeutic relating releases all the power that could pass between human beings. The gospel makes possible a different kind of relating, a profound and powerful kind of relating that I call *connecting*.

I earlier suggested that connecting occurs when the life of Christ in me touches the life of Christ in you. We know we have connected when our urges to do good have been strengthened by our time together. We know we have connected deeply when those good urges compete successfully with our bad urges, when we find ourselves living by the Spirit and therefore not gratifying the desires of the flesh (Gal. 5:16).

But how does this happen? How does the life of Christ in a parent, which is the only power for good inside any of us, get released so that it nourishes the work God is doing inside the disrespectful or insecure or arrogantly confident child—or in a ten-year-old overweight girl? What is the bridge that draws the life of Christ out of one person's heart and carries it across the distance between two people into the deepest recesses of the other person's heart?

The question is important to every spouse, parent, friend, pastor, and counselor. It gets at the core of what community is about. It addresses the real reasons why good people relate to each other. It has to do with what we most want to do—enter into a relationship of mutual soul care.

At this point, let me answer the question with three thoughts:

1. When a vision of what another person is and could become because of Christ is the fundamental passion behind all our efforts to relate, powerful connecting occurs.

2. As connecting occurs, wisdom develops: wisdom to discern what biblical principles need to be applied and wisdom to recognize the emotional pain and selfish motives that should be explored in order to promote richer trust and deeper repentance.

3. Powerful relating consists of grasping a vision of what God has in mind for someone and the faith to believe that the vision could become reality. A godly vision generates an excruciating sorrow when someone moves away from that vision, but that sorrow never eliminates hope or leads to disdain. And a godly vision releases giddy excitement when someone moves toward it, even just a little.

That's the simple idea. When the gospel enables us to believe that something terrific is alive in another and that something terrifically alive in us could actually touch it, good things happen. We accept people for who they are, we grieve over every failure to live out their true identity, and no matter what happens, we continue to believe in what they could become without demanding that it happen on our timetable or for our sakes, or that we play a big part in making it happen.[1]

Believing in each other because of the gospel: It's a simple idea that can be rescued from simplistic romantic optimism by watching it emerge from the mystery of the Trinity. Let's see how that happens.

CONNECTING WITHIN THE TRINITY

Nothing is more fundamental to appreciating the essence of Christian living than to ponder the implications of a central but often neglected truth: We have all been created by an Eternal Community of three fully connected persons. When we're told that we bear God's image, we immediately know two things.

1. *We were designed to connect with others:* Connecting is life. Loneliness is the ultimate horror. In connecting with God, we gain life. In connecting with others, we nourish and experience that life as we freely share it. Rugged individualism, proud independence, and chosen isolation violate the nature of our existence as much as trying to breathe under water. The capacities that distinguish us as human beings from all other creations (including angels and animals) were given to us so we could connect with each other the way the three divine persons connect. We have the capacity to enjoy the wonder of a relationship built on grace that no angel has ever personally experienced (fallen angels are not forgiven and unfallen ones don't need to be). Combine that capacity with the capacities to think, imagine, aspire, choose, and feel, and you have people built for trinitarian-like community.

2. *Connecting with others depends on using our capacity to relate for the enjoyment and enhancement of someone other than ourselves.* Paul said that he struggled on behalf of others with the energy of Christ

that powerfully worked in him (Col. 1:29). The life of Christ is coming out of me only when I am gladly ruled by a passion to know you, to bless you, and to be known by you so that together we can enjoy fellowship with Christ and with each other.

Trinitarianism teaches us that connecting is as vital to the life of our souls as blood is to physical life. When it's missing, we are ruled by the need to get it. Sometimes we settle for too little. Sometimes we conclude we'll never find it and become hollow people, mere shells carrying on our lives in quiet despair.

The story is told of a cancer patient who had a standing weekly appointment with his doctor for chemotherapy, a single injection that took a few seconds to administer. After each treatment, the patient would talk with his doctor for fifteen minutes. That fifteen minutes soon became the only time when he could speak about extremely painful matters to someone who understood and wouldn't retreat from the conversation.

Eventually, the patient began to suspect that the chemotherapy was no longer helping him and suggested to the oncologist that the treatments be stopped. The doctor immediately stiffened and said, "If you stop receiving chemotherapy, there is nothing more I can do for you."

The patient then decided to continue the weekly injections "in order to have those few moments of connection with his doctor."

The woman who told this story is a physician/counselor who added this postscript. This man's "oncologist was one of my patients. Week after week, from the depths of a chronic depression this physician would tell me that no one cared about him, he didn't matter to anyone, he was just another white coat in the hospital, a mortgage payment to his wife, a tuition check to his son."[2]

Some people settle for too little connecting. Others decide there is none, at least not for them, and retreat to empty living.

Why is connecting so important? Why do people pay such a high price (like continuing on with ineffective medical treatment) for even a moment of it? Why do people so often betray their families for a more intense experience of connection, even when they know it's illusory? Why are people with everything but connection eventually confronted by their own misery?

The answer to all these questions is the same: *because God exists as a community of connected persons.* We were fashioned by a God whose deepest joy is connection with himself, a God who created us to enjoy the pleasure he enjoys by connecting supremely with him but also with each other. To experience the joy of connection is life; to not experience it is death to our souls, death to our deepest desires, death to everything that makes us human.

Without a vision, however, without some sense of what God is up to in another person's life, there can be no true connection. How that idea develops as an implication of God's triune existence is my subject in the next chapter.

CHAPTER 7

Vision in the Highest

Think for a moment about that infinite stretch of time before anything was created. If everything created had a beginning, then there must have been a past eternity when there were no galaxies, no angels, no earth, no fish, no birds, no people, no anything—only God. Let your imagination wonder what it must have been like for God to exist with no one and nothing else.

This may be an exercise like counting angels on the head of a pin, but it does take the mind in interesting directions.

I've asked several audiences to close their eyes and try to think about a past eternity when there was only God and to then reduce to a single word whatever comes to their minds. Many words have been suggested, most commonly *majesty, awesome, peaceful,* and *harmony.* A few folks have come up with *boredom* and *loneliness.*

My word is *fun.* Let me explain.

Imagine the sheer delight of enjoying perfect relationships with two others with no fear of things turning sour, a community of three cut from the same fabric yet unmistakably distinct. Imagine three who, without a hint of competitiveness, are absolutely thrilled with the uniqueness of the other two, who will stop at nothing to give each other the opportunity to display their special glory. Imagine a community without even the shadow of evil, with nothing but perfect goodness, where every member can be fully himself without fear of promoting rivalry or releasing something bad.

57

What the Scriptures reveal about relationships within the Trinity since creation support these kinds of imaginings. The Father intends to bring all things under Christ and to give Him a name above every name. The Son has no greater delight than pleasing the Father. The Spirit loves to whisper "Abba" to fatherless children and to present Christ as the perfect lover to the unloved and unlovable. The trite phrase "One for all and all for one" becomes rich when applied to the Trinity. And the cynical phrase "Two's company, three's a crowd" doesn't fit.

Press the limits of your imagination a bit further. Ask yourself what it would be like for you to be a part of that kind of community—and the word *fun*, deeply understood, might come to mind. Visualize God's joy in *being* that community, and you catch a glimpse of what it must have been like to be only God. Add a group too large to number who enter that community without messing it up, without even the possibility of messing it up, and you find yourself looking at heaven as if through a telescope. It's far off, you can't see it with the naked eye, you can't really experience it, but you know it's there.

Now, come back to the present, to the time we inhabit between creation and consummation, to this lengthy moment between two eternities. Think how it all began.

After creating angels, the sun, moon, and earth and all the animals, birds, and fish, after sending rebellious angels away where they organized themselves into a powerful enemy, the Eternal Community called a meeting and said:

> "Let's create creatures with the capacity to fully enjoy us. We're absolutely happy with ourselves, of course, because who we are and how we relate is incomparably wonderful. But so far, we've created no one who can share deeply in the unique joys of an intimate relationship with us where we hold nothing back. Let's create personal beings like us to whom we can reveal the very depths of our glorious nature.
>
> "We must, of course, take into account what that will require. These new beings must be built with the freedom to love us and thereby experience the life of connection or to love themselves more

and experience the misery of disconnection. They will, of course, make the wrong choice. We will design them to enjoy the depths of our grace. But that will make them vulnerable to the enemy's temptation to want more than we can give them in their unfallen state, to long for grace that cannot yet be revealed. They will, therefore, believe the lie that we're holding out something good that they could find through their own efforts. But we can work their faithless choice to our advantage. It will give us the opportunity to reveal what otherwise would remain hidden, that we are *so* good and our love is *so* profound that we will sacrifice the joy of our community in order to welcome them into community.

"Son, at just the right time I'll send you to become one of them and to accept the guilt for their sin. Then (and here the Father's voice broke) I'll break our connection and let you experience the death of separation from me that all sin deserves. When they see the extremes to which we will go to bring them into our community, the yearning we'll build into their hearts to be loved like that will draw them back to loving us fully and trusting us with their very souls."

"Father, what you ask is painful beyond description to even contemplate. I cannot imagine what the actual experience will be like of not seeing your face. And yet I am delighted with your plan. It will give me the chance to let people see how wonderful you are. The joy of seeing you glorified makes it worth it all. There is no other way?"

"No."

"Then I will go, gladly."

"Spirit, you will come upon various people who will advance my purposes until my Son dies as a man and is resurrected. Then you will take up residence in every one you have drawn to me, and you will incline their hearts toward loving me so that obedience will become a joy and not mere duty."

"It will be my incomparable thrill to advance your purposes and to create within all those who accept your gracious offer of forgiveness an appetite to know you. And I will nurture that appetite until it becomes stronger than all others. I will not rest until they live in my strength and overcome all desires to find life apart from you."

"It's time to get started. Let's see what we can do with this bit of
clay. I have a vision for what it could become."

When there was only God, the Eternal Community was having fun.
Their purpose in creating people was to invite us to the party. As C. S.
Lewis put it, the serious business of heaven is joy.

Now, notice this. *The way they go about getting us to the party indicates
how keenly they had a vision for each other,* how deeply they appreciated
each other and the role each could play in their great plan.

The Gospels offer a fascinating glimpse into the Father's vision for the
Son and how passionately he appreciated the Son as he lived out that
vision. As I devote the next few pages to studying this glimpse, think
about our Lord's prayer that we would relate to one another the same way
the Father and Son relate. It might excite us with the possibility of developing a vision for one another.

The Gospels record three occasions during the Son's lifetime on earth
when the Father pulled back the curtain of heaven and space, twice
directly to our Lord, once on his behalf.

Occasion #1:   Jesus' baptism (Matt. 3:13–17; Mark 1:9–13;
                Luke 3:21–22)
Occasion #2:   Jesus' transfiguration (Matt. 17:1–13; Mark 9:2–13;
                Luke 9:28–36)
Occasion #3:   When a few curious Greeks wanted to get acquainted
                with Jesus (John 12:20–28)

It's interesting to note that all three occasions occurred during the
years of Jesus' active ministry, the last three years of his life. For the first
thirty years, from his birth to his baptism, the Father was silent.

And yet we know that during all that time there was never a moment
when Jesus failed to fully please his Father. Why didn't the Father speak out
during Jesus' childhood or adolescence? The question becomes intriguing
when you consider what it must have been like to see a perfect teenager.

When our kids were young, family devotions sometimes took the
form of one person impersonating a biblical character and the rest of

the family having to guess his identity. When our son Ken was about eight, he stormed into the living room in role.

"I hate having him for a brother," he loudly complained. "Mother never blames him for anything. If we get into a fight, mom always knows it's my fault. The other day I stole a dollar off Dad's dresser. They didn't even suspect him. When Dad realized some money was missing, he came to me and asked if I took it. 'No,' I lied, 'but I saw my brother take it.'"

"Son, that just couldn't be. You're not telling the truth. You must have stolen it."

Without any context, Kep, Rachael, and I were stumped. Ken then announced, "I'm Jesus' brother."

Of course! Jesus *never* stole a dollar from Joseph. He was sinless. And he never sassed Mary. He never grabbed the last cookie. Why then did his heavenly Father not speak out in loving affirmation during all those years?

Consider the first occasion that prompted a divine declaration from heaven: Jesus' baptism.

OCCASION #1

When Adam sinned, God's plan, to reveal that all goodness was found in him and nowhere else, began to unfold. Sin began when the suspicion was raised that God wasn't good, that there might be an advantage to looking for something better than God. From that point, the center of God's plan was to disclose his character through a person, someone we could look at and say, "So *that's* what God is like!"

For centuries, God had little to work with. Moses? Good man, but there is that matter of hitting the rock. David? Genuine passion for God, but a few major lapses. Daniel? Nothing visibly wrong, just not good enough.

And then came Jesus, rising up out of the waters of baptism, a man who had never sinned, who never *wanted* to sin. And he was praying, probably (though we're not told) dedicating himself to the task of giving people a good look at God.[1]

At that point, I picture the Father overcome with emotion, ripping open the heavens and, with sobs of delight, shouting: "You are my son whom I love. With you I am well pleased!"

If C. S. Lewis were commenting on this scene, he might have said, "Aslan's afoot!" Can you feel the passion pouring out of the Father as he sees the vision of Christ that was developed before the foundation of the world being realized?

When our older son Kep was nine, he was already showing signs of exceptional athletic talent. With a generous supply of hair so blond it was almost white, he would race up and down the soccer field with impressive agility. One day, I was by myself on the sidelines of a match, standing a few feet away from three other dads that I didn't know. The ball was bumping among a few dozen frantic feet near our team's goal when all of a sudden, one boy emerged from the pack with the ball clearly under his control. With white hair blowing in the wind, this boy sprinted the length of the field with the ball obeying his every movement. With a feint to his right, then another to his left, he powerfully kicked the ball right past the opponent's bewildered goalie.

I overheard one of the three fathers ask, "Who is *that* kid?" I cleared my throat, expanded my chest, took a step in their direction, and said, "That's my boy!" And then I added, "Genetics show!"

Multiply my passion a thousandfold, purge it of all corruption, and you have a small idea of what the Father said to Jesus. "That's my boy! Genetics show! You're just like me, an exact representation. When people watch the way you love and suffer, they will see a perfect picture of my heart. My vision of what you would become is now being realized. Son, *I love you!*"

OCCASION #2

The second shout from heaven was addressed to Peter on the Mount of Transfiguration. The man with no beauty that we should be impressed, to the natural eye an unremarkable Jewish carpenter, was suddenly revealed to Peter, James, and John in all the glory of deity; something like the Queen of England, dressed as a maid receiving coats from dinner guests, disappearing for a moment, then reappearing in regal attire with the queen's crown on her head. That might shake up the crowd a bit.

Then, if that weren't enough, Moses and Elijah showed up, apparently recognizable to the disciples, and they began talking with Jesus about his impending death.

Peter was overcome. Understandably, he didn't know what to say. Why he felt compelled to say anything argues for the oft neglected virtue of silence. Yet, at the same time, at least he spoke. Most men run from confusion into passivity and risk nothing.

Peter took the risk of speaking. But what he said was awful. "This is like nothing I've ever seen. We can't let it pass. I've got an idea. Jesus, let's celebrate you and Moses and Elijah by building three monuments, one in honor of each of you."

I picture the Father shuddering with divine exasperation as he shouted: "This is my Son whom I love!" And then he added, "Listen to him!"

Hear the Father's heartbeat. "Peter, if you celebrate Moses, you're putting yourself back under the law. And the law condemns you. You just can't do what it requires. That same law condemns everyone, including Moses and Elijah. But not Jesus. He has kept the law in every point. When he dies, he will bear the condemnation you deserve. No one else can do that for you. Peter, celebrate only Jesus. *Listen to him.* He has the words of eternal life."

From before Eden, the Father had a vision of what the Son would become when he lived sinlessly then died a sinner's death. And as he watched that vision unfold, it stirred him to deep passion. The first two shouts from heaven reflect that passion of the Father for the Son.

The third shout reflects the same passion but also lets us see the Son's passion for the Father.

OCCASION #3

In John 12:20–28, we're told that a few Greeks, intrigued by what they had heard of this miracle-working Jewish prophet, approached Philip to request a meeting with Jesus. Apparently, they wanted to learn just who this man really was.

Philip found Andrew, told him of the request, and together they went to Jesus.

Now when people I know ask me to meet with a friend of theirs, I reply in one of several ways. I sometimes say, "Sure, I'd love to. Could we meet at the bagel shop on Bowles Avenue at about three this afternoon?" Or I might say, "Can't do it today, but next Monday might work." Too often I am forced to reply, "I'm afraid my schedule is packed. I really can't do it. Sorry." Any one of these responses would be understandable and socially appropriate.

But listen to what Jesus said when Philip and Andrew asked if he could meet with a few travelers from Greece.

"The hour has come for the Son of Man to be glorified" (v. 23). What did that have to do with the request? Can you imagine Philip and Andrew exchanging a confused look? What's he talking about? Did we say something wrong? Maybe he didn't hear us.

Jesus continued: "I tell you the truth, unless a kernel of wheat falls to the ground and dies, it remains only a single seed. But if it dies, it produces many seeds" (v. 24). What does a lesson in farming have to do with a request to meet a few strangers? "The man who loves his life will lose it, while the man who hates his life in this world will keep it for eternal life" (v. 25).

Our two sons have always thought I could preach a sermon to them with no obvious trigger. And they were right (at least a few times) in saying to themselves, "Here he goes again."

But we must never say that about Jesus. If his words don't seem to fit the occasion, we simply aren't seeing something important.

After a moment, Jesus turned his eyes away from Philip and Andrew toward heaven. He was looking at his Father. To him he said, "Now my heart is troubled, and what shall I say? 'Father, save me from this hour?' No, it was for this very reason I came to this hour" (v. 27).

For what reason? "Father, *glorify your name!*" (v. 28). Can you hear it? "What I am about to do will let people catch a vision of who you are, and when they see you, how can they resist wanting you with all their hearts? Some Greek folks want to see me. And see me they will, hanging on a cross, dying, then buried, and raised up in order to bring with me a host of Jews and Gentiles, anyone who believes I came from the Father to bear his judgment against their sin. When people see me crucified, buried, and resurrected, they will see you in all your fatherly compassion, and they will no longer be afraid. The thought of even a moment of separation from you troubles my soul beyond words but there's no other way for people to know who you really are. Father, *glorify your name!"*

And the third time a voice came from heaven: "I have glorified it, and I will glorify it again" (v. 28 RSV).

Jesus had a vision of the Father. He saw into the depths of the Father's heart. And he was willing to pay any price to give us a similar glimpse.

In his next to last private conversation with the Father before he died, Jesus expressed his desire that we, his followers, would build a community among ourselves that would be like the relationship he and his Father enjoyed.

What would it be like if we had a vision for each other, if we could see the lost glory in ourselves, our family, and our friends? What would the effect on your sons or daughters be if they realized that you were caught up with the possibilities of restored glory, of what they could become— not successful, talented, good-looking, or rich but kind, strong, and self-assured, fully alive.

When people connect with each other on the basis of a vision for who they are and what they could become; when we see in others what little of Jesus has already begun to form beneath the insecurity, fear, and pride; when we long beyond anything else to see that little bit of Jesus develop and mature; then something is released from within us that has the power to form more of Jesus within them. That power is the life of Christ, carried into another soul across the bridge of our vision for them, a life that touches the life in another with nourishing power. Vision for others both bridges the distance between two souls and triggers the release of the power within us.

Before they worry about what they should say or do, before they explore the roots of their own emotions, the parents of the overweight ten-year-old girl need to reflect on their vision for their daughter. Are they more worried than hopeful? Does their vision for her rise no higher than a thinner body or the recovery of self-esteem? Or can they see the big picture, that nothing can ever happen to their child that God's Spirit cannot use to nourish the life of Christ within her? If they set their sights on cooperating with whatever God is up to, they will sorrow deeply over their daughter's pain while remaining mysteriously calm.

And their calmness will speak volumes to her. "You know what I'm going through and you really care. But you're at peace? What am I missing here?"

They will enter into her suffering without being absorbed by it. And they will still expect her to live responsibly in spite of her pain—not retreating to her room but staying involved with the family, not watching television instead of completing her homework, not plotting revenge on her taunting schoolmates.

As they continue to require responsible behavior, they will do so with the conviction that what is most deeply alive in their daughter actually *wants* to live responsibly. And they can be helped to sense their own *freedom* to love their daughter wisely if a friend believes that beneath their fear, confusion, and anger there exists a life in them that can be released toward the struggling girl.

Exactly what is the power within us waiting to be released? That's the question we've been pondering for several chapters. Perhaps now we can state the answer in a few simple words.

It is the actual life of God, the energy with which the Father and Son relate to each other, a set of inclinations put in our hearts by the Spirit and kept alive by his presence. It is a power that is most fully released as we develop a compelling and awe-inspiring vision of who another person is and what he or she could become because of the gospel.

Connecting is a kind of relating that happens when the powerful life of Christ in one person meets the good life of Christ in another. What every Christian can pour into another is the powerful passion of acceptance, a passion that flows out of the center of the gospel, a passion that fills the heart of God.

And the good in every Christian's soul waiting to be released beneath all the emotional and selfish rubble is the longing to be relationally holy, the urge to bless, to turn the other cheek, to live responsibly, to suffer well, to hope, to rejoice during hard times. And that set of urges, which controlled every moment of Jesus' life as he lived on earth, has been given to us in the gospel.

In the next chapter, I continue thinking about the powerful and begin to think about the good.

CHAPTER 8

What's Good about Us?

eople experience the life-changing force of healing relationships when *something powerful* comes out of one and touches *something good* in another.

But it doesn't happen very often; sometimes it does in a good marriage, occasionally with a few close friends, but rarely does it characterize a whole community.

This morning I listened to a gentle and talented man describe how shelved he feels in his local church. He doesn't know how to speak with the leadership about his hurt. He's not sure what is powerful in him that could come out or what is good in the leadership that needs to be touched.

Yesterday I spoke with a sensitive father whose son, during the past year, has moved from furious rebellion to genuine faith. He is a different person. Their relationship is vastly improved. "But still," the father told me, "I feel so awkward with my son. We just don't connect as I know we could."

Use the word connection lightly and you will report many experiences of it. Use it richly, and you'll feel lonely.

But still it's possible. Something powerful is in every believer's heart that could be poured out to touch something good that, by God's grace, is waiting to be released from every Christian's life.

What is powerful? What is good? Can we catch a vision of what could be that will keep us struggling toward deeper community no matter how frustrating and difficult the journey may be, no matter how often our failures try to persuade us that real connection is a pipe dream?

In the last chapter, I suggested that the "something powerful" waiting to pour out of every Christian's soul is the actual life of Christ. We must be clear. This is not merely an inspiring metaphor. When we become Christians, we are not only forgiven, we are also indwelt; we are not only acquitted, we are also empowered. Like a doctor pouring healthy blood into an anemic body, God's Spirit pours the motivation and energy of Christ into the veins of our soul. Something terrible is removed (the wrath of God) and something wonderful is given (the life of Christ).

Our hearts are enlivened with the same passions that ruled unopposed in Jesus' life, motives and desires and ambitions that were perfectly expressed in every choice he made, every word he spoke, every emotion he felt. They are alive in our makeup, rooted so deeply in the soil of our redeemed nature that, though they can be suppressed, they can never be destroyed. We are alive, in Christ. That truth is bigger news than we realize.

Although these new passions are the actual life of Christ, and although they represent the motivation that keeps the Trinity functioning as a perfect community, they do not, of course, elevate us to the status of deity. We do not *become* Christ, (he is truly one of a kind) but we can become *like* Christ. By the miracle of the new birth, we are restored to our dignity as human beings, enabled to uniquely reflect God to a watching world, to make the Father's character known as Jesus did during his life on earth, though not nearly as well. We are not an exact image.

The affections, passions, and inclinations that consistently prompted Christ have been given to us so that we might reflect the character of God primarily in the way we relate. In conversation with his father, Jesus said that the glory he had received from his father had been given to his followers so that they may be one (John 17:22).

The conclusion needs clear statement: *Something powerful has been placed within us that we are to release toward others in a way that promotes godly community.*

But there is a problem. The good power has competition. In Jesus' nature, that life had no rival. When pure evil met pure goodness in the temptation of Christ, the evil found nothing in Jesus that resonated. Everything in him, everything about him, was absolutely good. He could afford to "be himself" without risking mistakes.

Not so with us. Christ's life is in us, but so is something else, something different—and bad. And more often than not, the bad seems more natural, more basic to our real nature, than the good. It is therefore dangerous business to live by the pleasant-sounding standard "Be yourself." What we may judge to be a godly impulse could be its opposite. And that fact complicates the simple idea of releasing the powerful life of Christ in our relationships. Discernment is required. Let me illustrate.

A close friend recently shared a significant burden with me concerning his teenage son. I know the family well. I love them. For three days, I couldn't stop thinking about the problem. Was the Spirit directing my mind on their behalf? Or was I being obsessive? I didn't know.

During my ruminations, some thoughts occurred to me that seemed potentially helpful. Should I call my friend and share them? Did they reflect the passion and wisdom of Christ in me? Or were they the product of an active mind that proudly enjoys displaying its wares? If the second, they would have little power for good.

After three days of internal fussing, I felt even more strongly inclined to call. So I fussed some more. Were my inclinations more good (loving and wise) than bad or more bad (proud and self-serving) than good? Was I kindly suggesting a thought or two for his consideration or rudely intruding with a demand to be heard?

Jesus never had to wrestle with questions like these. We do.

So how do we know whether we're prompted by the energy of Christ or a less noble motive? Part of the answer is this: *We must discern what is deepest within us as we examine our hearts in God's presence, open to the input of godly friends and prayerfully meditating on appropriate Scripture.* We can assume that what is most deeply lodged in our motives and remains unshaken through prayer, counsel, and meditation is of God.

For two hours, I prayed, pondered, and perused Scripture. I spoke with my wife. At one point, as she prayed, I experienced a quiet confidence:

Love, not selfishness, *was* inclining me to call. I was convinced. So I called.

It went well. Something powerful met something good. As I shared my heart and mind, his heart received me with trusting gratitude, his mind moved toward his son, and his soul rested, I think, a little more in God. It was a good moment of connection.

I could share many stories, however, where it didn't work out so happily, where I had an edge to my voice, where a friend felt defensive or courteously indifferent. Why? Why do we so often fail to make connection? Why do we so commonly conclude that the effort isn't worth it, that keeping our distance from one another is the only way to avoid open division?

For connection to occur, something powerful must touch something good. Before we ask what is good in another that we can touch, we must think about why our words are so rarely powerful, why they so often fail to penetrate through the tangled defenses that surround the good.

Let me suggest a core principle. Whether our words reach through the bad dynamics in another's sinful heart and touch the holy appetites beneath depends largely on the answer to this: *Are we so empowered by the gospel that we are disposed to continue believing in another's miraculously granted goodness, and to therefore find delight in the other, no matter what degree of ugliness we encounter?*

When I sense that you want to discover what's wrong with me and change me, I will either slide into passivity ("Go ahead! Fix me!") or raise myself up to an arrogant height ("I can handle things. I'll consider what you say, but I'll make sure I don't buy all of it!"). But when I know that you love me, that you believe in me, that you recognize something terrific in me that you long to see more released, I'm more inclined to receive you, to let you pour into my life.

That's what happened in a conversation with Brennan Manning. Sometime ago, I had opportunity to chat with Brennan, my friend and writer of profound books on the spiritual life. During our conversation, I impulsively blurted out, "Brennan, I want time with you to talk seriously about something in my life. I need your help." Always gracious, Brennan immediately agreed.

I later wondered what had triggered that unplanned spontaneous request. It's true that I was plagued by a certain internal battle and that I deeply respect and love Brennan, but I hadn't intended to ask him for help. The request simply appeared.

As I reflected further, two memories returned. Several years earlier, Brennan had told me of his spiritual director's curious habit. Whenever he saw Brennan after an extended absence, he jumped up and down with delight.

I remember smiling. I pictured an elderly gentleman walking down a deserted beach toward an agreed upon meeting point and, spotting Brennan from a distance, hopping three or four times. The image amused me. It also drew me.

A year later, my wife Rachael and I tumbled out of a crowded elevator into a hotel lobby teeming with conference participants. Across the way, I caught a glimpse of Brennan's white hair and unmistakable smile. As I leaned toward Rachael to tell her I had just seen Brennan, he turned and saw us. Immediately, he jumped up and down. I was warmed to the bottom of my heart.

When those two memories returned, I understood my unexpected plea for help. I could trust a man who delighted in me.

Is that a small picture of what Paul meant when he told us to accept each other the way Christ accepts us (Rom. 15:7)? Does Jesus delight every time I come to him in prayer? As I write these words, my father-in-law has been in heaven for eight days. Did Christ jump up and down when Howard Lankford walked through the gates?

Luke tells us that the martyr Stephen saw Jesus *standing* at the right hand of God just before he died (Acts 7:55–56). But Jesus' usual posture is *sitting*. Was he getting ready to welcome Stephen home with a jump of delight?

A man who delights in you manages to see what is good beneath the bad. When I made known an ugly struggle to Brennan, his eyes moistened as he said, "Larry, I am so drawn to Christ because of you."

I was puzzled. He was drawn to Christ by a man who had just revealed his wickedness? I asked why.

"Because," Brennan replied, eyes still moist, "you are so troubled by whatever gets in the way of your relationship with Christ."

Brennan believed in me. The powerful life of Christ poured out of him and found something good in me that the Spirit had put there. Another moment of connection. I left that conversation singing.

When the gracious love of Christ, which delights in his children, is the energy behind our movement toward another person, something powerful is released. But that's only half of connecting. The powerful must meet the good. The question must now be asked: Exactly what is it that's good about us?

Is there a good beneath the obvious bad that exceeds the goodness of the kind non-Christian? Like many others, I've been burned by trusting Christian carpenters or mechanics or dentists to the point where I sometimes prefer an honorable pagan to do my work. Is there really something terrific in Christians, beneath all our obvious flaws, that is not present in unbelievers? If so, what is it?

WHAT'S THE GOOD WE'RE LOOKING FOR?

Let me begin my discussion by posing two questions.

1. What if the root problem in a Christian's life, beneath all the personal, emotional, and spiritual struggles, is *unreleased goodness?*

   - Not psychological disorder

   - Not emotional baggage from dysfunctional backgrounds and buried traumatic memories

   - Not hidden conflicts in our psyche

   - Not irresponsible living

But rather, a supernatural goodness within us that at any moment is not as released as it could be, a goodness that can be located and envisioned in its released form.

2. What if the central obstacle to releasing the goodness is already released badness?

- Not poor self-esteem

- Not a fear of giving ourselves that depends on earlier painful experiences

- Not a lack of motivation

- Not undisciplined habits

But rather, a badness within us that we neither recognize nor resist as we could (and should).

The answer to both questions, I believe, is yes: Unreleased goodness is our biggest problem and released badness is the most serious hindrance to releasing our goodness. We must therefore learn to *resist the bad* (a process the Puritans called mortifying the flesh) and to *release the good* (what they called vivifying the spirit).

It is the central thesis of this book that Christian community was given to us by God to provide indispensable assistance in doing both tasks. To understand how connecting (something powerful meeting something good) helps us mortify our bad inclinations and vivify our good ones, we need to understand two important things:

1. The center of a biblical theory of personality is the idea of two sets of urges within us, good passions and bad passions, bad passions that exist because of the fall, good ones that are reliably present under the new covenant.

2. God deals with our bad passions and good passions in a way we are expected to imitate; connecting with another Christian involves doing for each other, as we struggle with our internal civil war, what God does.

Good Urges and Bad Urges

Jonathan Edwards devoted an entire book to developing the idea that out of our hearts come good affections and bad affections. "The affections are of two sorts," he writes in his old English style. "They are those by which the soul is carried out to what is in view ... (maturity); or those by which it is averse from it, and opposes it. Of the former sort are love, desire, hope, joy, gratitude, complacence. Of the latter kind are hatred, fear, anger, grief, and such like."[1]

Although his style of expression belongs to an earlier day, what he says does not. We know what he is talking about. The Christian businessman retires early to his hotel room after a difficult day of meetings. One press of the button and pornography will fill the television screen. He knows the battle between good urges and bad urges. He calls his wife, gets some work done, writes to his married son, then goes to sleep. He never presses the button.

The next day, his meetings go well, exceptionally well. That evening, the bad urges seem unaccountably stronger. He yields.

He is obsessed with why after a bad day he had victory and after a good day he failed. Is there value in figuring it out?

Whatever the complexity may be, it is clear that we are a strange mixture of good urges and bad urges, and that these urges seem to have a life of their own. The bad urges in non-Christians, it should be noted, sink no lower than the bad ones in Christians, but the good ones don't reach as high. Without God's Spirit, the best we can do is to be kindly selfish. As John Owen said, "The only reason why an unregenerate man is not under the perpetual pursuit of some lust is because he is distracted by so many more of them."[2]

With God's Spirit, we can love as Jesus did, but we can also sin like the devil. Indwelling sin is a lifelong problem. Indwelling goodness is a lifelong reality awaiting release.

How did we get to be this way? To understand the good and bad urges within us, go back to the beginning when there were neither, when Adam and Eve were innocent, uncorrupted but not energized by the deepest passion of God. Until that fateful time by the tree, they lived in simple dependence on God, the only being they knew who had been kind to them.

Then someone else appeared who suggested that God might not be as good as they supposed. "Have you ever wondered," the serpent asked Eve, "if there might be something good *outside* of God that could be enjoyed if you had the sense to go after it?"

Adam knew the serpent's idea was wrong, but when Eve ate the forbidden fruit and became a lawbreaker, perhaps he wondered if there was enough goodness *inside* God for him to somehow restore a criminal to a place at the family table. Could he do it? Would he even want to? If Adam trusted God, he might lose his wife. Would God forgive her?

Surely God couldn't be that *good.* And with that doubt, Adam disconnected himself from God, unaware of the incredible mess he was setting loose.

Drastic consequences follow when a creature breaks away from the creator. For Adam, the immediate consequence was terror. "Can I go back? Does he hate me? I stand exposed as one who broke the one command God gave. I can't bear to see his eyes. I must look away. I'll make it on my own. Let's see, what resources do I have for taking hold of my life?"

So Adam, and all his descendants with him, struck out on his own, independent from God, dependent on self, all because he did not believe God could be *that* good. We have all since committed ourselves to seeing how we can manage without connecting with a God we don't fully trust.

But disconnecting from God does not work well. It requires that we deny anything in our makeup that depends on connecting with God. We therefore deny the deepest longings in our souls, longings to love a God who loves us and to love others the way God loves us. We want that, but without God we can't have it. To fully embrace the desire of our hearts when there is no possibility of satisfaction creates intolerable misery. Better to acknowledge only those desires for which we can arrange satisfaction without God.

We also disconnect from the inbuilt sense of right and wrong that now condemns us. To bow before justice spells our doom. Against the yardstick of ultimate morality we fall hopelessly short. We regularly break God's law. Better to shorten the yardstick to match our moral height. Then we can feel more comfortable.

It now comes naturally to blunt our awareness of what we were designed to enjoy and how we were intended to live. We are disconnected, not only from God, but also from ourselves, from our strongest desires and our moral compass.

Disconnection from Self	Denied Longings	Justified Selfishness	I'll get what I can!
Disconnection from God	Unbelief: He Can't Be *That* Good!		Independence from God/ Dependence on Self

Committed to managing life without God and afraid to face our emptiness and guilt, we see what we can do. Two questions immediately present themselves: Do I have what it takes? Will people cooperate with my efforts?

We experience fear (maybe I don't have what it takes), rage (it's just not fair that I am not be able to get what I need), and demandingness (someone better come through!).

We're scared, mad, and demanding as we enter the experiences of life. Our highest goal is that we "make it," that we experience some level of internal satisfaction. Over the course of thousands of learning experiences, we settle into a basic life strategy, continuing to do whatever creates personal pleasure and working hard to avoid whatever brings pain.

Our lives become thoroughly and strategically self-centered. Whatever kindness we extend or responsibility we show is prompted by the hope of personal advantage. No one is taking care of us as we want to be taken care of, so we look after ourselves. We therefore never connect. Nothing comes out of us that is aimed at arousing the good in another. Every choice is in the service of self. We are slaves to sin.

Our disconnection is complete. We find ourselves separated from God, ourselves, and others. We are foolishly independent, unaware of our destiny and purpose, committed to a justice that revolves around us, scared that we're inadequate, desperately insecure, angry when things don't go our way, consistently demanding that they do, incapable of loving anybody and not terribly bothered that we don't, finally alone with ourselves, either settling for lesser satisfactions and "doing fine" or troubled by any one of dozens of symptoms of our terrified, angry, selfish internal life. The sketch can now be completed. I call it: "The Flesh or Our Old Heart."

To illustrate the sketch, consider a man's struggle with pornography. His personal problem is sex addiction.

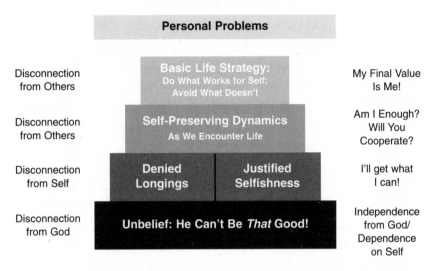

The Flesh
or
The Old Heart

	Personal Problems	
Disconnection from Others	**Basic Life Strategy:** Do What Works for Self: Avoid What Doesn't	My Final Value Is Me!
Disconnection from Others	**Self-Preserving Dynamics** As We Encounter Life	Am I Enough? Will You Cooperate?
Disconnection from Self	**Denied Longings** / **Justified Selfishness**	I'll get what I can!
Disconnection from God	**Unbelief: He Can't Be *That* Good!**	Independence from God/ Dependence on Self

God declares that there is no goodness in sex outside the boundaries of a loving relationship with a lifelong mate. When we believe him and therefore are inclined to do what he says, obedience yields a joy that supports us in whatever frustration may exist.

Connecting to God opens up the depth of our longings and helps us realize that any sexual pleasure that fails to express our love for God and for another is no more satisfying than cotton candy. And we sense the rightness of the law forbidding it. We *want* to keep the law. We're connected to ourselves as longing beings designed to live within boundaries.

But consider the disconnected man. Communion with God means nothing. It isn't felt, tasted, or experienced. At best, it is a transitory Sunday morning happening that lasts till the closing hymn. That man senses a void that yearns to be filled but lacks the sense to realize that he longs for love, not pleasure. And he knows no compelling reason why the pursuit of pleasure should be judged as wrong. He has lost touch with his humanity, with his longing for love, and with his moral design.

Experience with life teaches him that no one is especially interested in his well-being. Perhaps he discovers few talents within himself or opportunities that reliably provide him with a taste of the satisfaction he craves. While keeping up appearances as a responsible, good man, he inwardly gives up on relationships or achievement as a means of finding what he wants. His capacity for sexual pleasure, intended to provide a physical excitement that more deeply bonds him to his wife, becomes, in the absence of connection with her, the means of experiencing nothing more than a moment of predictable pleasure. Because sexual excitement from pornography becomes the closest thing in his experience to soul satisfaction, because it seems justified and reliable, and because it provides pleasure without risk, it becomes the center of his life. Lust controls him. He is a sex addict.

The cause of his addiction is released badness, wrong desires that are honored, urges that result from disconnecting, first from God, then from self and others. The cure, as we shall see, is released goodness coupled with a commitment to resist the badness, both empowered by connecting.

In our natural state, before the new birth, we all walked in the lusts of our flesh. That was our only option. Our entire approach to life was built on the conviction that God wasn't good enough to fully trust. The root of all our choices therefore was self-dependence, self-interest, self-preoccupation, the exact opposite of the choices that govern relationships within the Trinity. We were filled with bad urges. "Every inclination of the thoughts of his heart was only evil all the time" (Gen. 6:5).

However, Christians are no longer in their natural state. In all believers' motivational reservoirs there is another set of inclinations that comprise what the Bible calls our spirit, our new nature. From our flesh come only bad urges. But from our spirits good urges flow. Let's look at this second set of inclinations.

One theologian speaks of our "dramatic new creaturehood," which is the result of God's passion for "welding man's inmost self . . . to the holy will of God." Since Jesus' death and Resurrection, God has established a new arrangement with his people, a New Covenant that "moves beyond Sinai by lifting spiritual inwardness to a new dimension."[3]

Under the terms of the New Covenant, God not only provides forgiveness for everything bad within us, but he also plants a new source of goodness within us from which we may draw. The goodness he grants consists of an appetite for holiness, a desire to relate well. These good urges, because they come from God, are potentially stronger than every bad urge. That means that within the heart of a betrayed wife or a discouraged businessman or a lonely single lies a passion to forgive, to continue on responsibly, to give to others—passions that could become stronger than urges for revenge, escape, or momentary gratification.

Moving through our emotional struggles and handling relationships well require that we tap into the good urges within us to strengthen and release them. The New Covenant is, I believe, the most neglected and most pivotal doctrine in shaping our approach to personal growth and to connected relationships. We are now defined by something terrific no matter how severely we have been hurt or how badly we fail. At any moment, we have something wonderful and powerful to give to others and to release in ourselves.

But we spend too much time exploring our badness, dwelling on our pain, and understanding the darkness within us in hopes of weakening our unruly passions. Or we disregard the mess as nothing but an opportunity for excuse making and exhort people to live up to good standards. Neither approach properly takes into account the state of affairs brought about by the New Covenant.

Under the old covenant, God's law was outside of us, like a speed-limit sign, telling us what to do. But, like teenagers in a new sports car, we weren't inclined to obey the law. We saw the sign as a limitation on our fun, not a provision for our safety.

When Dad handed over the keys, he firmly instructed us to completely stop at stop signs, pass only with clear visibility, and drive within the posted speed limit. We told him that we would do exactly what he said. When God thundered from Sinai, the Israelites told Moses, "Tell us whatever the Lord our God tells you. We will listen and obey."

God, with the same sad headshake of so many fathers, said to Moses, "I have heard what this people said to you. Everything they said was good. Oh, that their hearts would be inclined to fear me and keep all my commands always" (Deut. 5:28–29). Within days, the Israelites broke every law God had given. The teenager was caught speeding.

In effect, God was saying, "Their words are good, but their hearts aren't in them. My people are ruled by an urge in the depths of their being to disregard my law in favor of contrary desires. They do not know me well enough to *want* to obey me. They still see my law as a damper on their fun."

They were fleshly people, governed by desires that exist when God is not fully trusted. Their doubting, self-ruled nature had no serious rival. They lived in accordance with the flesh.

God dealt with these people according to a simple arrangement. He gave them the keys to their lives, handed them a manual called Ten Rules of the Road, and promised to reward them if they followed the rules completely and to punish them for any infraction. That was the old covenant.

It was fair. God had every right to command obedience. The law was good. There was only one problem. People weren't particularly inclined to do what they were told. They did not know God well enough to be overwhelmed by his kindness or to see every choice to obey as an opportunity for joy. Keeping the car within the speed limit felt like sacrificing real pleasure.

The old covenant didn't do the job; it couldn't change people's hearts (Heb. 8:7). People's hearts were not right. The urge to rebel was firmly embedded in their core motivation. The law merely exposed the rebellious urge. It never changed it or replaced it with a better one. So God introduced a New Covenant. It began with a fuller revelation of God than had ever been given before. He really is *that* good, so good that for one hideous moment he broke up the eternal triune community in order to bring us into its pleasures. The center of the New Covenant is the fuller revelation of God as forgiving and gracious, relentlessly determined to do whatever it takes to give us the fun he originally intended us to enjoy.

"They will all know me," God declared. And "I will put my laws in their minds/and write them on their hearts" (Heb. 8:10). In another place, he announced his plan to give us new hearts, ones that wanted to obey (Ezek. 36:26–27).

God never fixed our old hearts. He never sorted through the complexity of our bad urges to trace the events that shaped them. He simply gave us new hearts, by letting us see the depths of his kindness (he is *that* good; he jumps up and down when sinners turn to him) and by writing the Ten Rules of the Road into our makeup so that following them would become an expression of who we are rather than merely an effort to do what we should.

A New Heart
The Spirit
Where Good Urges Come From

Faithfulness Through Trials

Connection with Others — Basic Life Strategy: Yield to the Good; Resist the Bad — My Final Value Is God! He's the Point

Connection with Others — Spiritual (Self-Denying) Dynamics As We Meet Life — My Adequacy Is in Christ I'm Here to Give

Connection with Self — Embraced Longings | Godly Conscience — I Want to Live for Him

Connection with God — Belief: He Is *That* Good! — Dependent on God for Life

The Flesh
or
The Old Heart
Where Bad Urges Come From

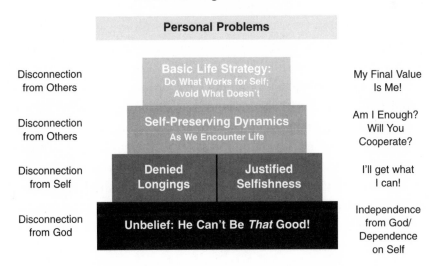

Personal Problems

Disconnection from Others — Basic Life Strategy: Do What Works for Self; Avoid What Doesn't — My Final Value Is Me!

Disconnection from Others — Self-Preserving Dynamics As We Encounter Life — Am I Enough? Will You Cooperate?

Disconnection from Self — Denied Longings | Justified Selfishness — I'll get what I can!

Disconnection from God — Unbelief: He Can't Be *That* Good! — Independence from God/ Dependence on Self

Christians now have two sets of inclinations, bad urges coming out of our flesh and good urges arising from our new hearts, the spirit that God has put within us. And the good urges, because they represent the creative work of God, are stronger, at least potentially, than every bad urge.

That's who we are, people who at the same time want to do good and want to do bad. What then should we do? Fix something? Try harder to do right?

I pray for the day when Christians (including me) will do the hard work of learning to jump up and down for our friends, our mates, our children, even when they are irritating, when the life of Christ will be released from our hearts to awaken hope in the people we love. I want to encourage older Christians to believe they have something wonderful to give that only years can supply; I want to see them enter meaningfully into the lives of younger people and be well received as their elders, their shepherds, their spiritual guides. And I want to see them honored for doing so.

Most simply, I want us to connect, as friends with a handful, as shepherds with a few.

I've already suggested that there is a power waiting to be released from each Christian's heart that could connect with the goodness in another's. If the connection consists of profound acceptance, looking for the good, and the ability to see bad without retreating, then friendship exists, a relationship that can bear the weight of advice, rebuke, and failure and richly enjoy the pleasures of encouragement, shared interests, and laughter.

If, however, the connection goes beyond acceptance to include penetrating wisdom and spiritual discernment, then friendship has deepened into shepherding. Shepherds not only jump up and down at the sight of another, they also spot the Spirit's bright work in the darkest recesses of a regenerate soul. And they have a knack for surfacing both deeply hidden ugliness without becoming disdainful and terrifying pain without collapsing. This sort of wisdom and gentle discernment is given only to saints who seek God through the worst anguish and who learn to yield cherished dreams to God's purposes.

Communities of shepherds and friends, relationships where wisdom is more appreciated than threatening and where acceptance is felt more than criticism, where single moms pour good things into their difficult children, where husbands touch the most sensitive parts of their wives' abused souls, where friends make an eternal difference in each other's lives: That's my vision.

As I try to bring the vision into focus, questions flood my mind:

- Is connecting happening?

- Do we think connecting is happening when it isn't? Is there such a thing as false connecting?

- Are happy families and good friends relating powerfully or merely pleasantly? What's the difference?

- Why do so many well-intentioned families disintegrate into a war zone and so many strong friendships end?

- Does significant connecting occur more commonly in counseling offices than in Christian communities? If so (and I think it does), why? Why don't more Christian communities address the deep issues of the soul? Is the problem a lack of training?

- Could counselors help? Could they provide a meaningful perspective to elders and pastors that could enrich their ministries?

- Why are godly trained counselors often different from godly church elders? Why would I prefer to tell my personal story to any one of a dozen counselors I know than to most elders I've met? Shouldn't elders be shepherds? Why are most of them business managers? The folks I'm most willing to share myself with are nonintrusively compassionate, they listen well, they offer wisdom I trust, they think deeply about the human condition, they know their Bibles, their authority comes more from their character than credentials, and they keep confidences. I know that describes a good Christian counselor, but shouldn't it describe an elder?

The questions run on, but one thread ties them together: *Something is getting in the way of connecting in our Christian relationships.* Something good is waiting to be released, but something bad too often sneaks out instead, something that may look good but is deadly to our relationships. What is it and what can we do about it? Let's think about that.

CHAPTER 9

The Enemy Within

Something's getting in the way of connecting. If releasing people into rich community is God's purpose, we can assume that God's enemy is creating some obstacles. That enemy is presented in the Bible as a trinity: the *world* (any system of thought without Christ at the center, a system that is deceptively attractive), the *flesh* (inclinations to trust anyone but God for life, inclinations that are fueled by a deceived mind that thinks God is not good enough to trust), and the *devil* (God's most personal enemy, the villainous leader of fallen angels who is unalterably committed to opposing God at every turn, especially to spoiling God's plan to win a community of followers who love him and in whom he finds pure delight).

God's strategy for overcoming our enemy (particularly the flesh, our most internal enemy) involves such hard to understand ideas as dying to sin (Rom. 6:2), dying to the law (Rom. 7:4), being released from the law to serve in the new way of the Spirit (Rom. 7:6), yielding ourselves as instruments of righteousness (Rom. 6:13), living by the Spirit (Gal. 5:16), putting to death whatever belongs to our earthly nature (Col. 3:5), mortifying the misdeeds of the body (Rom. 8:13), clothing ourselves with virtue (Col. 3:12), not conforming to this world but being transformed by renewing our minds (Rom. 12:2), and resisting the devil by standing firm in the faith (1 Pet. 5:9).

All of these commands, and so many more, emerge from two core ideas: We live out the gospel by killing an already defeated enemy and

85

surrendering ourselves to the energy and prompting of the Holy Spirit in our new hearts. Or, to put it in terms we've already introduced, we are to mortify the flesh and vivify the Spirit.

My focus for the next several chapters will be to understand what we need to mortify and what it means to put to death a conquered enemy. (In the last few chapters, we'll take a look at what we can revive and release.) Something within us must die, and we must be the executioners. We are not to let it live while we try to behave better. We are given no hope that if we understand its roots and development, it will slink away like a defanged lion and cause no more trouble. We are to grab it by the neck and throttle it and throttle it again every time it shows up, knowing there will always be something to throttle till we get home. But what are we to choke and what does choking it look like?

If we're to relegate the do-what's-right model to its proper place on the periphery, if we're to discount a therapeutic model that thinks exploring the bad and the ugly will somehow fix it or make it disappear, and if we're going to be there when the geyser erupts, when the living water gushes forth from those newly dug springs within us, we must reckon with the bad urges that are already trickling into our lives and polluting everything we do. Let's consider the obstacles to connecting, the enemy within.

James asks whether both fresh water and salt water can flow from the same spring (James 3:11), using a metaphor to teach that bad passions come from one nature and good passions arise from another. We're never told to kill either the world or the devil. God will one day burn down the world and lock up the devil. But he's told us to get on with the job of putting to death the enemy within us, the enemy who is so much a part of who we are that we often mistake him for a friend, or worse, as our true self.

Think with me about what it is we're supposed to kill and how we can go about doing so. Three brief illustrations will set the stage.

It took effort, but she managed to keep smiling. Only the most insensitive could miss the tears filling the reservoirs behind her frantic eyes.

"I listened to what you had to say," she began. I had just presented a short talk on connecting.

"I really want to connect with my son—he's sixteen—but it never turns out right. I go home from church or a seminar on loving the unlovable, and I'm all charged up. But within minutes of seeing him, it's all gone. I don't feel powerful at all. I'm more angry and hurt than anything else, and that's what comes out of me. I have no idea what it means to release the energy of Christ toward my son."

She paused to regain control, then continued. "It is so hard to see any good in him at all. Sometimes he's less obnoxious, occasionally even pleasant, but I don't see anything really good to touch. He got saved at camp seven years ago. I don't know if it just didn't take or his new nature is hidden beneath all this mess or what. I want to connect with him, but I just can't. I more often scream at him or just ignore him to keep the peace."

What's the problem? What's the problem *in her*—not in her son, but in her? Is it ignorance? Does she need instruction from an expert on handling power struggles? Would training her in the skills of resolving conflict prove helpful?

Would presenting her with another way to do it "right" release her to reflect Christ to her boy?

Or is her anger and sense of failure rooted in profound dependency needs that began years ago with a rejecting father and were more recently heightened by a nasty divorce? Is therapy appropriate to surface the buried conflicts triggered by her disagreeable son, to help her see that two-thirds of her anger is really directed at a cold father and an abandoning husband?

Something's getting in the way of her providing the opportunity for connecting with her son. What is it? What could her community do to help?

Another parent, this one the father of a thirty-year-old woman, stared blankly at the wall as we chatted in his hotel room. He was a picture of defeat, the life knocked out of him.

"I can't reach my daughter," he said flatly. "She's living with her boyfriend, the third one in eight years, and she's about to give birth. It's our first grandchild. My wife can't even talk about our daughter, let alone to her. I have no idea what we'll do as grandparents.

"I thought we had a great relationship when she was a little girl, and all the way through her teens. I thought we connected well. Maybe we never did. The only vision I have for my daughter now is watching her sink even deeper into sin and getting more and more hardened and distant from us and God. I know that's not much faith, but that's where I am. I don't know if I'm more heartbroken, guilty, or numb. I have no idea what to do. Just pray, I guess."

Is there really a power inside this man that could awaken a thirst in his daughter for what her image-bearing soul most deeply desires? If so, what's blocking its release? What would you tell him? Would you give him advice? Refer him to a family therapist? Offer to pray and ask him once or twice a month how things are? Or could something powerful in you touch something good in him? Do you have a vision of how a Spirit-filled man would operate in this situation? Could you encourage movement toward that vision? Is there something *in you* blocking that movement that you must first deal with?

One more story. They had been friends for several years, close friends. But Brad had felt Steve slowly pulling away for about a year. The phone rang less often with a cheery "let's-go-out-for-coffee" message; a gray cloud had settled over their friendship, leaving a chill.

It was true that Brad felt critical of Steve for a few things and, perhaps unwisely, had mentioned his concerns about a year ago. Is that what had started the problem? Was Steve hurt? Offended?

Maybe there was no problem. Maybe Steve really hadn't pulled away at all. When Brad asked Steve if there was anything wrong, Steve warmly denied any conflict. "It's our crazy schedule," he insisted. "I'd love to get together more often. *I miss you!*"

Brad had to admit he was a bit insecure and tended to require more than his share of affirmation. Maybe it was all his imagination. That possibility made him reluctant to press Steve to more thoroughly discuss the tensions Brad felt. The relationship slowly deteriorated into a series of occasional "great to see you; we need to get together" exchanges. Brad felt empty and confused.

When relationships sour, our best efforts don't seem to reproduce what has been lost or generate what we desire. Even Paul and Barnabas had their problems.

Should Brad write off his friendship with Steve as one of those relationships which functionally die for reasons unknown? Should he get on with whatever other opportunities for connecting exist, wait to reconnect with Steve in heaven, do his best to stay cordial and supportive till then, and remain open to whatever more might miraculously develop now?

I tell these stories for the same reason premarital counselors might show pictures of beautiful weddings to the engaged couple and then present a dozen snapshots of dirty kitchens, screaming kids, a desk piled high with bills, and a couple staring coldly at each other.

We've painted a picture of connection. We've caught a glimpse of the perfect community in action. We've indicated what Christ has done to make it possible for us to enter into community with him and to connect with each other, to touch something good with something powerful.

It sounds wonderful. It *is* wonderful. It just doesn't happen very often. And we have to face that fact.

God did. The incarnation stands as the supreme example of leaving the palace to work in the slums, of leaving perfect community to introduce connection to a bunch of disconnected people who didn't even know how badly they wanted it and, incredibly, fought against it.

It's not that we're stupid, in the sense of a limited intellect. Our problem is foolishness. Foolishness is neither ignorance nor mental dullness. It is the product of deception. Foolishness sees what's bad and calls it good and looks at something good and finds it unattractive. That's *moral* stupidity.

That's why it's sometimes so hard to know what to kill. The Bible tells us what the fruit of our sinful nature looks like, but when we see it in our lives at a particular moment, it doesn't always look so bad. Bad urges seem reasonable, justified, necessary, even good—certainly not worthy of death. The inclinations of the flesh promise life if we yield to them, and for a while they deliver.

So we think about them, try to understand them, negotiate with them, find what is useful in them, and indulge them to see what happens. And we end up slaves to the flesh. Why? Because they seem to work.

Let me illustrate. One of the kindest men I know is also one of the loneliest. He met a young lady in great need. His kind heart was deeply touched. With no conscious thought of romance, he provided her with substantial help out of his considerable resources.

Her warm appreciation touched his lonely heart. Kindness turned into a longing for more. He felt urgent desires to move beyond friendship to romance. The romantic passions felt, to him, entirely legitimate (well, nearly so). They struck me as a demand for relief coming more out of the flesh. I told him what I thought. He didn't agree. He felt good as he pursued her, hopeful, excited, alive.

In her mind, however, romance wasn't part of the original deal. When he made clear his intentions, she felt set up, used, betrayed. The relationship ended unhappily for both. He recently commented, "I can see now that my lonely heart, from the beginning, was demanding an opportunity to receive love. My kindness was extended in the service of that demand." Had he recognized that earlier, he might have spent less time walking in the flesh and reaping its painful consequences.

The flesh, the enemy within, dons a friendly uniform, one that a Christian might wear, and suggests reasonable directions. We welcome him into our ranks. When he causes trouble, we try to whip him into shape, get him to cooperate with the program, and stop interfering with our efforts to do things right. Or we work hard to figure him out. What makes him tick? Why does he demand gratification *that* way? Maybe a journey into the past will uncover the source of these crazy tendencies and enable us to reason more effectively with him.

What we need to do, of course, is shoot him. Naive Christians, the kind who want to freely release the goodness within them and trust their hearts to lead them aright, do not want to enter the battle raging in their souls. They have no appetite for identifying and destroying the enemy. Spiritual warfare, they hope, will involve only light skirmishes, never a fight-till-someone-dies conflict.

Obsessive Christians, on the other hand, spend more time studying the enemy than fighting him. Specialists in understanding sin can describe how every hurtful experience from your childhood has impacted you, how you've dissociated, self-hated, and idolized false gods, all in the service of running from God. Obsessives listen carefully and take notes.

For them, understanding their insides becomes a never-ending pursuit, energized by the hope that gaining insight into the dynamics of the flesh will somehow weaken its power, or give them better control over it.

Thoughtfully aware Christians, however, neither naive nor obsessed, know that the enemy must be identified and identified carefully. The disguise must be ripped away, the horror of the enemy's ugliness and the pain he creates must be seen, not to understand the ugliness, not to endlessly study the pain, but to shoot the enemy.

And if he doesn't stay dead, we must shoot him again, then beat him, then tie him down in the sand under a hot desert sun, turn loose an army of red ants on his body and walk away without sympathy. And then we must do it again and again and again, till we're home. An overdone metaphor? Not when we see the enemy for who he is, for what he wants to do. We are at war, the enemy within is the flesh, and he wants to ruin our relationships and thwart God's plan.

If we don't hate the enemy, we'll hate something or someone else. The mother will hate her disrespectful son or herself or her divorced husband or God—until she identifies the real enemy.

As I write this chapter, I'm behind deadline. My publishers are more than gracious, but I like to be on time. I thought I'd make it, but (and here come the excuses, which I prefer to call reasons) a string of illnesses, my father-in-law's death, and responsibilities I agreed to months ago that now are bunching up are keeping me from my yellow writer's pad. (I've heard some writers have departed from biblical tradition and now use computers.)

Add to that my chronic struggle with author insecurity. (Do I have anything to say? If what I'm saying is true, why is it not doing more for me? Have I read widely enough to treat my subject thoroughly?), and the battle rages.

Tonight, I came unglued. Pressure won. I lost. Anger roared out of me toward *myself* (Why was I so stupid to agree to all these responsibilities?), toward *others* (Why don't people cooperate more with my need to find large chunks of writing time?), toward *life* (It's just too tough to live outside the garden; what will go wrong next?), toward *God* (He could be a tad more sensitive to my needs; what would it cost him to make me physically healthier?).

Ever been there? What do you do? Some just sulk. Many try harder to get their spiritual and personal lives in shape. Not a few find therapists to see what's really wrong.

But ask a question that's not in fashion, a question that too often remains unasked: What would it mean to mortify the flesh, to shoot the enemy, to resist bad urges? And then realize that to answer that question, we must first ask and answer another: What needs to be put to death? What am I to kill? The answer, of course, is the flesh, that nature within me inclined to sin. But what is it? How do I recognize it?

As a start, think of it this way: *Sin is any effort to make life work without absolute dependence on God.* It is giving higher priority to my satisfaction than to God's pleasure, it involves a follow-up commitment to find joy for my soul outside of God, a commitment rooted in the belief that there is something truly good that God does not provide. It boils down to self-dependence and self-preoccupation and self-centeredness, attitudes that look to other people and things for the satisfaction we were designed to enjoy. It is looking at God and saying, "No!" or, worse, dismissing him as we would a bellhop after he's carried our bags to the room.

Sin is independence, a rebellion against God's authority based on disbelief in his goodness, an independence that creates agendas for our lives that run directly counter to his. Scripture identifies at least four sinful agendas that enliven the flesh:

1. Depending on your own resources to make life work

2. Reducing the mystery of life to manageable strategies and following them

3. Making it a priority to minimize personal risk

4. Finding satisfaction wherever you can

In the next few chapters, we'll study the biblical basis for asserting that these four agendas (among others) are sinful, and we'll discuss how each one creates a passion that must be killed. We'll also see how these passions provide an opportunity for false connecting, even among sincere believers.

As I sat unglued a few hours ago, frantic, fuming, wondering how best to inform my publisher that I had given up on writing this book, I had little choice but to admit something was wrong. (Strange that such an obvious fact requires acknowledgment, something like saying, "Oh yes, there is an elephant in our living room.")

From there, I could see that I was not experiencing spiritual fruit. The flesh had the upper hand. But what was I to do? Do I just put away anger by saying "Anger, be gone!"?

Or do I realize that what I thought for years was a friend is in fact a good thing that has somehow ended up in the service of the enemy? My ability to think, to conceptualize, felt threatened as I worked on the book. That threat provoked such a strong reaction because my abilities mattered too much. I was depending on them to make life work: bad agenda #1.

I chastened myself for being so poorly read. If I were more familiar with the spiritual classics, if I had more carefully studied Romans and Galatians, then all would be clear, and I'd know exactly what to write: bad agenda #2—knowing exactly what you're doing at all times; reducing life to a workable plan. If you follow it, congratulate yourself; if you don't, a good whipping is in order.

And writing this book will invite dialogue, some of it critical. Do I really want to put in print what I believe, what the Holy Spirit seems to be teaching me? Maybe I should tone it down a bit, make my ideas more palatable, say what I almost mean: bad agenda #3—minimizing risk.

I felt empty, scared, discontent. I wanted to grab a sandwich, a cookie, maybe watch an hour of television. I *deserve* it: bad agenda #4—finding satisfaction wherever you can, preferably quickly, on demand.

Four agendas, each with their urges pressing me to find something good apart from God, urges that are self-defeating, weakening, vision denying: I must tell them to go back to hell where they came from and where they belong. But what does that mean? How do I do that?

I thought about what I believed, or claimed to believe. Christ has laid out a pattern of good works for me that he provides the adequacy to complete. His Spirit will prompt me to move in the direction he chooses to send me. I am told to abandon myself to him and believe that whatever happens—bad reviews, ministry failure, serious illness, restricted opportunities for service, disappointing relationships—will not only *not* interfere with his purpose for my life, but they will actually also further it. He promises true satisfaction if I abide in him. The urges growing out of those beliefs lead me in a different direction from the others, the bad ones.

Until I discern what must be challenged and destroyed and stir up what I know to be true, until I resist the bad urges that grow out of my wrong agendas and release the good urges that arise from my embraced convictions, I will live with neither joy nor meaning. I will connect with no one and allow no one to connect with me. I will experience disconnection.

But since I am inescapably hungry for connection, I will pursue a counterfeit. I will find others with whom I can moan. I will share my struggles with people who, like me, depend for life on their personal adequacy; and if we discover areas of mutual confidence we'll embark on a joint project and call it fellowship: bad agenda #1—*making life work*. Here we go again.

I'll find people who agree with me on how life should work, and we'll offer a seminar: bad agenda #2—*getting a plan that you can trust.*

I'll hang with people that are terrified of real risk but have the social competencies to successfully function without meaningful vulnerability, and I'll feel safe relating with them: bad agenda #3—*minimizing risk, playing it safe.*

I will be drawn to others who share my appetite for immediate relief. We'll build a relationship around the Chicago Bulls or a great restaurant or golf, or something worse: bad agenda #4—*feeling good quick.*

Our culture is built on false connections based on wrong agendas. The Christian community could be different. In order for the difference to be visible, we need to recognize the enemy within that urges us in wrong directions and offers a convincing and, for a while, satisfying counterfeit of connection. That enemy needs to be killed.

But how do I kill it? Do I need your help? Is mortifying the flesh a private battle, or should it be done in community? And how do I discern what is in me that needs to die without getting obsessed with my motives and preoccupied with my pain and sin? These are the questions I now take up.

CHAPTER 10

Dying Together to Live Together

Mortify the flesh, we're told. But what does it mean? We're supposed to kill something inside us, something that gets in the way of connecting. What is it, and how do we carry out the execution? In this chapter, I suggest that whatever it is and however we're to kill it, we're to deal with the problem together.

The center of the Christian life, we should remind ourselves, is not about killing anything. The *route* to life is death, but the *center* of life, the point of Christianity, is living together in the enjoyment of God. We die in order to live.

More than anything else, Christianity showcases the risen Christ. We're invited to know him, spend time with him, draw strength and encouragement from him, relax in his laughter when we expect him to yell, and serve him gladly because we genuinely like what he's up to.

Christianity is about the life of the Trinity released in human community. But the doorway into that life is death, and death is always painful. When Jesus died, he died alone. There is no greater pain. When we die to ourselves, we're to do it together, with our community. There is no stronger bonding.

The gospel informs us that God found a way to bring us out of the grave by putting Christ into it. When he walked out of his burial place, we walked out of ours, and we did it in his strength, with his invincible life flowing through our veins. Because of Christ's death and Resurrection, we're both forgiven and empowered, loved freely and enabled to love freely.

But there's a problem. The life of Christ is in us, but something else is too. We want to do good, but we also experience powerful urges to do bad. We are strongly inclined, among other things, to depend on ourselves and prove that we have something of value within us, to come up with a manageable plan to handle life's challenges, to protect ourselves from whatever might frustrate that plan, and to experience a sense of internal well-being that we were designed to enjoy. And these four sets of pressing passions lie behind our more visible problems.

We are all that "wretched man" that Paul described himself to be, a raging battleground between good and evil. Christ's death liberated God to do what he otherwise could not do, to forgive us completely for all the badness in us without compromising his justice (which, of course, he would never do). And it also built a funnel from God's heart into ours through which he could pour his life into us. The cornerstone of the gospel is Christ's death as the basis of our life.

But then, once we're Christians, we're told that we must die to ourselves, to the flesh that is still within us. We must put to death, again and again, everything in our souls that hinders the free expression of our new life.

In our eagerness to live, we sometimes forget that first we must die. To *become* Christians, we die with Christ, one time. We accept his death as the punishment our sins deserve. Most of us understand that.

But to *grow* as Christians, we must die to the flesh, repeatedly, daily, until we're home. At different times, the Spirit takes us through special seasons of accelerated dying, when the pain is especially acute. Following the lead of Saint John of the Cross, we aptly call these seasons "dark nights of the soul." It's that death to ourselves that we're more likely to forget or trivialize. But when we do, when we think about it only a little or assume it means nothing more than staying out of pornography shops or cutting back on gossip, we lose the power to connect.

Both deaths, Christ's death *for* our sin and our death *to* our sin, are difficult, Christ's immeasurably more so because he suffered absolute isolation from God so we would never have to. Only Christ could justifiably cry out, "My God, my God, why have you forsaken me?" (Matt. 27:46). He died the death that justice demanded, a death that for one awful afternoon disconnected him from the Father.

Our death to the flesh is entirely different. We die a death that grace enables, a death that disconnects us only from what is bad in order to connect us with everything good. But it doesn't feel that way. As we give up what we wrongly depend on to maintain our sense of well-being, we're dying to death, but it seems as though we're dying to life.

However, it's what we must do. We are instructed to die to the flesh, to identify, despise, confess, and resist whatever urges are within us that direct us to something or someone other than Christ for the experience of life. We don't bother much with that obligation these days, and we certainly don't think of dying to ourselves in the presence of another. The idea of mortifying the flesh with the discerning encouragement of spiritual community is more a relic from earlier, more primitive days than a present reality. What little effort we give to putting to death our sinful nature is carried out in private struggle; it's rarely community business.

Ever since the reformers properly reacted against the manipulative and heretical excesses of the medieval confessional, Protestants have tended to devalue and mostly abandon the practice of formal confession. A few moments once a month of private self-examination before receiving communion, for many a token and not terribly upsetting look at themselves, is about all that's left.

Those matters that need to be confessed, the secrets we harbor and the internal struggles we endure in our never-ending fight against sin, have been removed from church community and taken to the counselor's office. When we long to make ourselves known to someone who could represent Christ to us, when we look for a wise, caring person who will hear us and open us up with love rather than shut us down with rules or clichés, the few we find in the church (if we find anyone at all) are typically unavailable. So we turn to professionals, to people trained in "therapeutic relating" who are available because they make a living being available.

We've come to a time in our culture when therapists have been asked to take over the functions formerly handled by priests, a function that properly belongs to biblical elders who listen because they've had the courage to listen to their own hearts, to face what's bad and discern the Spirit, who can speak powerfully into the lives of others because they hear Christ speak powerfully into their lives. But these people are in hiding.

Their numbers are small. Their God-ordained function has been given to others.

C. G. Jung once observed that modern psychotherapy arose partly in response to the void in Christian community left by the Protestant insistence on *private* confession. We no longer struggle together with our deepest concerns and our most internal battles. Religion, we often hear, is a personal matter between us and God, where we keep our distance from others and relate openly with God. One difficulty with that philosophy is that we end up being less than honest with him as well.

We rarely share in a way that requires the gospel for the community to survive and for meaningful bonding to occur. The masks remain in place; we tell only parts of our stories; we deal (a bit proudly) with emotion-laden struggles that don't disturb our final commitment to independence; we find ways to connect that don't require the depths of Christian grace.

When we feel the need for richer connection, we unburden ourselves with a therapist. Confession, the practice of coming clean with someone whose gaze we invite, of dying to ourselves in the presence of another, has moved out of the church and into the counselor's office. Once there, it has often been secularized. Our internal worlds of envy, insecurity, fear, and greed have been stripped of their moral content and reintroduced as psychological dynamics, a set of forces that we "work through" rather than "die to."

We must ask why we no longer die to ourselves in community, why we so rarely journey from self-dependence through the valley of death to life in the Spirit in the presence of a connecting guide. Why is that journey replaced by a very different one, where with the help of a therapist we rearrange our self-dependence into a healthier, more effective pattern?

Where are the spiritual leaders, the shepherds of the flock, the elders of God's people? Why are one or two official Christian leaders assigned the job of pastor and expected to carry a burden that belongs on many shoulders? Where are the people who can listen well and guide us through our problems to the Father's heart and who regard it as their calling to do so? Whatever became of the idea that all believers are priests?

Our communities are filled with people desperate to unburden themselves in the presence of another, to be known at a level where the only antidote to disdain is grace, to sink beneath death's dark waters while in the grip of strong hands that promise to raise them up into newness of life.

In recent conversations, I've asked ten Christians if they had someone in their lives whose strength and wisdom encouraged them to make themselves fully known. All ten answered the same way: "I'd give my right arm to have someone like that in my life. There's so much going on inside me that I'd love to share, not to find answers necessarily but just so someone *knew*. But I have no one like that."

So where do we go when the need to have someone know us becomes strong? Often we find a culturally sanctioned priest, a professional elder, a counselor, someone more likely to explore the details and background of the psychological forces stirring within us in hopes of sorting them out (the "fix what's wrong" approach) than to identify the flesh in order to die to its power. Sometimes, of course, we seek out a "biblical" counselor and end up with little more than a set of instructions to follow (the "do it right" approach), where little connecting takes place.

Church communities offer few opportunities to die together; counseling professionals spend more time understanding what needs to die than they do killing it. The effect is that few Christians give serious attention to mortifying the flesh, to dying to ourselves in the presence of another in order to live together in trinitarian community.

At different times in church history, communities of believers have decided to deal with personal sin as a group. The record of what happened provides little encouragement to try again. Sin has been unwisely confessed too openly ("I confess my lust for your wife."), authoritarian leaders have arisen to pronounce judgment, people have become obsessed with ferreting out every trace of sin in themselves and others, and communities have been split, destroyed, and corrupted.

But still we must try. Scripture tells us to confess our faults to at least one other member of our community. The journey toward Christ is intended to be a group expedition where we walk together as honest strugglers who believe the end point is worth any hardship. We share the life of Christ together and are called to nourish that life in one another; *but we must also resist the urges of sin together.* We must not be alone when we enter the death experience of discovering that our flesh-inspired strategies for living no longer work. During those times, connecting provides hope that there is life after death and gives us the courage to mortify the flesh, to further abandon our efforts to find life apart from Christ.

As I write this book, I am moving through a season of death. I've talked about it with a few, mentioned it to audiences, and allude to it now in this book. But *talking* about dying with others is vastly different from *actually dying* in the presence of another.

God is stripping me of much that I've depended on for my sense of well-being. The effect is a struggle with self-doubt and with questions about my usefulness that at times are overwhelming. The process of dying, I've discovered, includes a period after the old props have been kicked away and before the new foundation can be felt beneath my feet. During that period, the soul is ripped apart, filled with desolation and despair, made raw, lacerated. It longs for a healing that no one can arrange. It is a season of absolute vulnerability before God. If he does nothing, there will be no Resurrection, only ongoing death, which no one can endure.

Only my wife knows the depths of my torment. And she *stays*. And a few friends are with me in the valley. A phone conversation with a friend connected me to his love. I found the courage to feel my despair when that conversation ended; the despair rose out of my depths and poured out in uncontrolled sobs. I allowed it to come, partly, I believe, because another friend was visiting with us and watching television in another room. He heard my tears, immediately switched off the television, came to where I was sitting, embraced me, and said nothing. I poured out my pain; he wept over my agony and prayed. I better understand what Henri Nouwen felt when Pere Thomas pulled Nouwen's head to his chest.

As he prayed, I knew that life was in me. I sensed it. I knew a richer experience of that life was ahead. I realized that the voices of darkness were not the only voices. I could see the unfulfilled agendas that were provoking my pain. I could hear the messages trying to persuade me that I have nothing to offer, that my failures define me, that my lack of freedom to simply be is a permanent condition. And I knew they were lies. I knew that because of Christ's death the pressure to be someone, to do better, to engage more effectively was no longer the basis of my life. For at least that moment, I could put to death all those agendas as inclinations that no longer defined me and therefore didn't need to control me. I could see them for what they were and see myself as destined for better things.

I have experienced death in the presence of my wife and a few friends. They have watched the process, they have fixed nothing and exhorted nothing, but they have poured into me the hope that death precedes life, that death to self is the route to finding oneself, that crucifixion means Resurrection is coming. Because we died together, because we connected during the experience of death, we now live together. We experience fellowship in Christ, the real thing that only he can provide.

The obstacle to connecting (the flesh) becomes our opportunity for deeper connecting when we recognize it and mortify it together.

If we are to seize that opportunity, we must become nonobsessively discerning, we must learn to recognize what needs to be mortified. In the next two chapters, I discuss four wrong agendas of the flesh to help us gain that discernment, to rid ourselves of the obstacles to deeper connecting.

CHAPTER 11

Urges to Be Killed

W hen *I want to connect,* so much else comes up inside me that gets in the way. I sometimes feel jealous, annoyed, indifferent, insecure—a whole range of self-preoccupied emotions—as I relate with someone. And that makes it difficult to pour something powerful out of my heart into a goodness I'm supposed to see in another.

Sometimes I experience a closeness that doesn't feel legitimate, a false connection, like the togetherness that gossips enjoy. It seems then that I'm enjoying myself by honoring bad urges that should be resisted.

Some urges within me are good. They should be identified, nourished, and released. Some are bad. They should be identified, starved, then killed. What are the bad ones? That's my subject in this chapter and the next.

I have noticed four metaphors in the Bible that highlight different activities of the flesh. Together, they have become a mirror in which I can see dirty smudges on my face, dirt that needs to be wiped clean, smudges I might otherwise not see. Or, without a good mirror that accurately reflects what is there, I might think of them as beauty marks. Bad urges are tricky. They can *look* so good.

And for a reason: Everything bad is a perversion of something good. Only God creates. And everything he creates is good. But goodness can be corrupted and has been, among both angels and people. Whatever is good has an attractive counterfeit. Sometimes the process of corruption creates a bad thing out of good by nudging aside a greater good.

Take sex, for example. In marriage, it is honorable, undefiled, and good. God delights when married couples enjoy each other sexually. But when the desire for sexual pleasure becomes central, when it becomes a higher priority than kindness and commitment, then it becomes bad.

We make one of two common mistakes in dealing with our selfish urges: Either we pay them too little attention and remain unaware of the danger they pose, or we pay them too much attention and frisk every choice we make for hidden bad motives. If we keep the mirror clean and look into it when the Spirit prompts us to, then perhaps we can err less on either side.

The following four metaphors correspond to the four agendas I mentioned in chapter 9. As an outline for this chapter and the next, let me list them and indicate the wrong agendas they point out.

1. *City building.* City builders depend on their own resources to make their lives work. Their commitment to personal *adequacy* gives rise to urges that block connections.

2. *Fire lighting.* Fire lighters reduce the mystery of life to manageable categories of understanding. These categories are useful to the degree they suggest strategies for handling life that have guaranteed outcomes. Their commitment to having *confidence* in their plans occupies them in ways that spoil connections.

3. *Wall whitewashing.* Wall whitewashers make it their priority to minimize risk, to protect themselves at all costs against whatever difficulties might frustrate their plans. Their commitment to *safety* restricts the freedom that connecting requires.

4. *Well digging.* Well diggers insist on feeling good, now and on their terms. They demand control over their internal experience of well-being. Their commitment to *satisfaction* on demand dulls their awareness of the impact they have on others as they seek their own pleasure. That lack of concern over their impact gets in the way of connecting.

Let me now discuss each metaphor and see if a mirror develops that reveals what is inside us that must be killed.

CITY-BUILDING: A COMMITMENT TO ADEQUACY

The Metaphor

When Cain killed Abel, God pronounced judgment, swift, clear, and firm. The last element in Cain's punishment, the one he reacted to most strongly, was, I think, the most severe. God told Cain that he would be "a restless wanderer on the earth" (Gen. 4:12), that he would never settle down in a neighborhood. Because he violated community, he was denied the joys of living in community.

His immediate response was to complain. To live without a home, to never lay down roots, to sleep every night in a different motel, to enjoy no long-term relationships was too much for him to even anticipate, let alone experience.

So Cain rebelled. Rather than accepting his punishment as deserved and then pleading for mercy, he determined to create the community he knew he wanted, no doubt honoring that desire as a legitimate longing. We're told that when his wife gave birth to their first son Enoch, Cain was busily working to *build a city* (4:17).

And he named it after his son (Enochville?), intending perhaps to establish an enduring legacy, to get for himself what God wouldn't give him. That's the spirit of city builders, to draw from their own resources in a determined effort to secure the advantages of life that God refuses to provide.

The theme runs throughout the Bible. Consider a brief sampling:

- Lamech's children laid the foundation of civilization. Jabal was a farmer, Jubal a musician, and Tubal-Cain an industrialist. The resources of a wicked man's family were used to begin organized human community (4:19–22).

- Nimrod was a man who lived "before the Lord" (10:9). That phrase suggests that God was keeping an eye on him, the way a parent specially observes a child likely to get into trouble. He was the first multiple city builder. Among his achievements was Babylon, the symbol throughout the Bible of worldly power (10:9–10).

- The people in Shinar held a meeting and said, "Come, let us build ourselves a city, with a tower that reaches to the heavens, so that we may make a name for ourselves and not be scattered over the face of the whole earth" (11:4). The city was never finished. God spoiled their plans by dividing their languages so they couldn't continue working together. Apparently, the city of Babel would have developed into a community God wouldn't like.

- The prophet Haggai took the Israelites to task for spending time and money on their own houses while the house of God sat unfinished (Hag. 1:3).

- Jesus knew his followers were troubled. They had given up opportunities for personal advantage to be with him, and they weren't sure what was ahead for them. Jesus comforted them by letting them know that he intended to build each of them a wonderful place to live. He did not tell them to build their own homes here. He promised only difficulties in this world but a home in the next (John 14:1–3).

  God beamed with delight over followers who "admitted that they were aliens and strangers on earth," who did nothing to relieve their homesickness but looked ahead to the city with foundations whose builder and architect is God. He declared that he was not ashamed to be called their God because "he has prepared a city for them" (Heb. 11:10, 13–16). The implication is hard to miss: *God is disappointed in followers who build their own cities here.*

- The Bible ends with a vision of a city, the Holy City "coming down out of heaven from God," a place with no death, mourning, tears, or pain (Rev. 21:2–4). God welcomes his family to enter it, live there forever, and enjoy its tree-lined streets, its cheery brightness (no clouds there), and its community of people who can't stop singing for joy. The apostle John sees what's ahead, he hears Jesus say, "I am coming soon," and, like a child who has been away at camp too long, he says, "Yes! Come, Lord Jesus. Take me home!"

The Meaning of the Metaphor

Now, put all that together. Start with a core truth: *The passion for home runs deep!* Ever since Adam and Eve were banished from Eden's comforts, ever since the first murderer was sentenced to living out of a suitcase, we have all been tormented with an unquenchable ache.

We want to go home. We dream of relaxing in a well-worn chair with all the bills paid; we long to enjoy our family gathered round the table with no one missing; we wish good friends would drop by and we'd have the time to welcome them for an evening of fun and conversation.

We want *shalom,* that neighborhood where everything is exactly the way it should be. Our urge for *shalom* is too strong to deny. It arises from depths within our hearts that define our nature. Nothing seems more legitimate than wanting a home.

But we're not there. Every minute makes it obvious we're somewhere else: health problems, money worries, relational tensions, emotional suffering. We're living in a world where nothing is exactly the way it should be. And God doesn't seem to be working to improve the situation.

We're not in hell; there are good things, even wonderful things that bring legitimate pleasure and joy. But what's bad makes it impossible to fully enjoy the good.

It's hard living here. We're not home, but with all our hearts, we wish we were. So we try to make where we are look as much like home as possible. When it becomes clear that God, the only one with the power to create *shalom,* is not devoting himself to making it happen now, with puzzled indignation we take on the job. Remember the old camp-style chorus?

> This world is not my home
> I'm just a'passing through
> My treasures are laid up
> Somewhere beyond the blue.
> The angels beckon me
> To heaven's open door,
> And I can't feel at home
> In this world anymore.

Many of us have rewritten it to read:

> This world is not my home
> But it will have to do,
> I'll do all that I can
> To make my dreams come true.
> The angels aren't much help
> They tell me what's ahead,
> But I don't like their plan
> Things must work now instead.

Now, notice what happens. As soon as we determine to enjoy this world as much as we can and decide that it's up to us to make things more comfortable, a question immediately grabs at us: *Can we do it?* Do we have the needed resources? Can we pull off a good marriage; will our spouses want us in ten years; will we want them? Are we capable of raising good kids, or will they break our hearts? Will we be successful; can we make enough money to decorate our worlds as we'd like? Is our giftedness sufficient to keep the church growing? Do we have what it takes to create lasting friendships; can anybody enjoy us for long once they get to know us?

When we commit ourselves to building our cities here, we are instantly consumed with doubts about our adequacy, with whether we can do the job we've accepted. *We then live to erase our doubts.* If we're successful, we feel proud and call it joy. If we fail, we learn to hate (ourselves for failing, others for not helping, God for his indifference) and feel justified in doing so.

You can tell a lot about people by finding out what they fear the most and what they hate the most. City builders are terrified of failure. They hate their own weaknesses. As they try to live in community, they are preoccupied with their own adequacy or lack of it, feeling either smug or empty. And they are coiled to erupt in fury against anyone who increases their fear.

I remember my early days in practice as a psychologist. The first time a prominent Christian referred a relative to me, I felt pressure. "Here's my chance. If this goes well, I'll be talked about in high circles. I'll establish a good reputation. Oh God, please help."

Understand, of course, those weren't the words I heard myself say. What I allowed myself to hear went more along these lines: "Dear Lord, it's such a burden for this Christian leader to worry so much about his son. If I could be effective with this young man then perhaps his dad's ministry could make even more of a difference for your kingdom. Please help me do a good job."

Even though I wrapped my fleshly urges in spiritual dress, I sensed that my prayer was not getting through. I wasn't convinced God was committed to my noble agenda. So I took inventory of my resources:

- I did well in graduate school.

- Several therapy supervisors predicted great things for me.

- Local word was already spreading that I was a pretty decent therapist.

Yes! I can do it. I think. I hope so. God, please! Help a little.

Paul spoke of struggling for others in the energy of Christ (Col. 1:19, 2:1). He longed to see others become more like Christ (Gal. 4:19). The apostle John jumped up and down with delight when the people he loved remained faithful to God (3 John 4). Their agenda was to build God's kingdom.

Mine was to build my city. I struggled for myself more than for my client, wringing my hands over whether good things would happen. Was I adequate to make them happen? That question burdened me more than whether the work of God's Spirit was being furthered in this young man's life.

The urge to help, though disguised as a good one, should have been killed. But I honored it. The man was helped. His dad was impressed; my reputation grew. The foundations of my city were firmly laid. Praise God! Or me! Whomever. I don't really care. My life was working. What else matters?

City builders don't connect. They require others to affirm their adequacy. And when someone does affirm them, a bond develops. False connecting occurs.

An acquaintance of mine began a parachurch ministry. It never quite grew to the size he envisioned, but it made its mark. It developed into a "significant" ministry with its own headquarters, a few branch offices, and a sizable staff. He hired key personnel who admired him and posed no threat to his leadership, men and women whose abilities could further his purposes. Those purposes, of course, were the mission statement of his ministry that expressed worthy spiritual intent.

When things went well, he was generous, joyful, and great to be around. When difficulties arose, something deep inside was threatened. Without knowing it, he became a fragile man. He withdrew from those who questioned him, citing concerns with loyalty to the mission, and clung to those who "believed" in him, which came to mean those who never confronted him. The inner team became a clique. Folks on the outside called it a cult.

God eventually dealt with this good man the way he often deals with his children who build cities. He took him to the desert, to a place where his talents were not enough to provide nourishment for his soul, to a place where the false connecting afforded by loyal staff couldn't relieve the pain. He sat in hot sand, alone, with neither the tools nor equipment to erect a shelter.

In the desert, God spoke tenderly to this man as he typically does (see Hos. 2:14).

> You have always thought your talents could bring you life. When you were elected president of the senior class at your Christian high school, your determination became firm to enjoy the opportunities for leadership your skills provided. You foolish child. I want you to live, not to merely enjoy the temporary pleasures of achievement. I designed you for relationship with me, a relationship where you are gladly dependent and I am enjoyed as fully sufficient. I'm not mad at you. I'm just grieved. Your heart is so empty and has been even when your ministry was going so well. The city you're building is nothing but a drafty shack. I want to shape you into a home for me, to be a wonderful dwelling place from which I can do my work. That's my agenda for now. And later, I'll bring you to my eternal home. Wait till you see the place that's under construction right now that I've already deeded to you.

For a while longer, though, you need some time in the desert. You must come to see that without me all your resources are useless. You can build a city now; you may get what you want, but it will bring leanness to your soul. I want you to realize that your resources are worthless when you devote them to your own purposes. They're dead. They cannot provide life. When the desert convinces you of that, you'll mortify the urge to prove your adequacy.

And then you'll discover another urge within you, one that can become even more powerful if you nourish it. And when that urge is released, I'll be thrilled, others will be blessed, and you'll be filled with joy.

It's all coming. Just a little while longer in the desert.

Desert experiences, those uncontrollable and unpredictable seasons in life when things that used to work just fine no longer work, are good. In the hands of a gracious God, their purpose is to change the questions we ask. Rather than wondering if we're adequate to keep things together and reach our goals, we begin to hear ourselves ask the question our new heart has been whispering all along: "I love my Lord. What can I give to his purposes?"

That's a question the Spirit delights to answer. He's the one who distributes gifts among the people of God to enable us to do our part in the body, to offer unique connection to others. Changing the question from *am I adequate?* to *what can I give?* is a slow, difficult process. But the urge beneath the wrong question must die so the urge to serve Christ can flourish.

The passion of a city builder to find, prove, and display personal adequacy dies best in the desert.

FIRE LIGHTING: A COMMITMENT TO CONFIDENCE

The Metaphor
Listen to the words of Isaiah:

> "Who among you fears the LORD
> and obeys the word of his servant?

Let him who walks in the dark,
who has no light,
trust in the name of the LORD
and rely on his God.
But now, all you who light fires
and provide yourselves with flaming torches,
go, walk in the light of your fires
and of the torches you have set ablaze.
This is what you shall receive from my hand:
You will lie down in torment." (Isa. 50:10–11)

There is an enormous difference between the *joy of discovery* and the *passion to explain*. The former gives life a sense of adventure. The latter makes us hate mystery.

God has created the world with an orderly structure that can be reasonably investigated and profitably used. The job of science is to understand that order as fully as possible.

But behind the structure is a person, a free, unmanageable person who is bound to nothing outside himself. It is therefore impossible to reduce all mystery to understandable categories. Some level of confusion must remain. If we trust the person behind the structure, that confusion becomes a source of adventure. If we don't trust him, we hate the confusion and try to get rid of it.

For those who enjoy discovery because they know a good God is moving through the chaos toward a wonderful conclusion, mystery poses no problem. It is welcomed. Explain what you can, and relax even when you can't. But for those ruled by a passion to explain, for those who insist on feeling confident in their own plans, mystery is offensive. They want to know exactly what they must do to provide for their economic future, to restore harmony in their relationships, to succeed in their career or ministry. Confusion is an enemy. Uncertainty is a challenge to overcome.

God's words through Isaiah tell us one way we can know if we are living in the flesh or in the Spirit. When we bump into something we can't explain, when we find ourselves in a dark tunnel and aren't sure how to get out, is our stronger impulse to trust God or figure out what to do? Do we quickly reach for a flashlight to help us see the road ahead? Or do we firmly grasp the hand of the only one who can see in the dark?

Where is our confidence—in God or in our ability to come up with a good plan? If we walk confidently in the light of our own torches, Isaiah informs us that we are not relying on God. The demand to walk a path with a predictable outcome is an urge of the flesh. It needs to die.

The Meaning of the Metaphor

Fire lighters love formulas. They live by them. When they can't devise their own, they turn to experts who confidently tell them what to do to achieve desired results.

When fire lighters try to help people, they are more concerned with doing it right than touching others' souls. They trust their model for helping more than the voice of God, more than the Spirit speaking through his Word into their redeemed hearts. Connecting is replaced by control. Fire lighters work too hard. They follow theory too closely; they depend too much on approved technique.

When our sons were in their early teens, I remember spending several hours one evening writing out my analysis of where they were in their development, determining what they needed to successfully move through the sociopsychological demands of that stage, and planning how I could best help them.

A few years later, when Kep was in the middle of his rebellion, I screamed at God, literally: "Tell me what to do, and I'll do it. *Just tell me what to do!*"

When he refused (I'm not sure what I thought he ought to have done), I consulted an adolescent specialist—actually two of them. "What should I do?" I demanded. "Do I ground him, sell his car, and require attendance at youth group? Or do I calmly discuss things with him, share my concerns, and reasonably explore options?"

Since God didn't answer those questions in the book he wrote, I lost interest in reading my Bible. Interesting how we prefer to see the Bible as a rule book, a collection of principles to follow when life gets rough, rather than as a revelation of God's heart. We prefer instructions on what to do over an invitation to connect our hearts with his and to then do whatever he reveals.

Fire lighters hate uncertainty. They are terrified of confusion. Their nagging question is always: "Am I right?" Am I doing this properly? Am I making big mistakes? Is there a better way of handling this situation? Who would know that might tell me? Fire lighters demand clear answers, practical instructions, and doable solutions. Life is livable if they can feel confident in their plans. So they insist on good plans and often find them in the Bible, not always because the plans are there, but because they want them to be there.

Parents of young children are especially prone to fire lighting. When they get together for mutual support, open sharing, prayer, Bible study, and discussion of good books on parenting, it can be a wonderful thing. But sometimes they gather in groups to intensely discuss the latest Christian manual on raising kids. If someone questions the approved text too strongly, the group's welcome is withdrawn. The parents' terror of confusion is covered over with an almost slavish confidence in what the experts recommend.

To sustain their confidence, they stick together. They report successes, affirm each others' faith when things don't work as hoped, and chide one another for lapses in following the plan. With a common flashlight illuminating the way, these scared people connect, falsely. Cultlike elements develop in their community. Agreement and conformity are more valued than debate and diversity, and all happen in the name of biblical truth. The passion to be right and their consensus on what is right becomes the foundation of their closeness.

But that passion and the question it inevitably spawns—Am I right?—come out of the flesh. The *demand* to be right, an insistence that we find confidence in a strategy because of its guaranteed outcome, is an urge to be killed. It must die because it replaces a final trust in God with confidence in a system we can follow.

God dealt with one expression of my fire-lighting passion the way he often does, by deepening the darkness. He allowed my confusion to get so thick that I was faced with only two options: Trust God or sink into despair. The darkness he permitted shattered my confidence in what I was doing and removed all hope of regaining confidence through a better plan.

During Kep's rebellion, not only did I write out a game plan for helping both Kep and Ken move smoothly through their developmental stages, but I also studied biblical stories to see what worked and what didn't (I spent hours in 1 Samuel 2 pondering Eli's failure with his two sons, Hophni and Phinehas). I read books by the reigning experts, and I prayed and fasted.

Because my core agenda was to be right and to know it, I could richly connect with no one. I was pouring very little into my wife, my sons, or my friends. I remained involved with them, often very kindly, but my core struggle was to be right, not to touch something good in another with whatever was spiritually alive within me.

The darkness deepened. God gave little opportunity for me to be confirmed that I was right. I became more confused. I fought the confusion; I hated it as all fire lighters do.

Then I received word that Kep had been expelled from college. Something became clear. There were no formulas. There were no right strategies with guaranteed outcomes. There was only God. Would I trust him and rely on his name (not as a new plan to get what I wanted)? Would I simply hold his hand, trust his heart, and move into the darkness with no purpose other than to reflect something of Christ? *Only deep darkness helped me to fear God more than confusion.*

When the lights go out, when our dreams shatter and there's no way to piece them back together, that's when our questions are most likely to change. No longer do we ask, "Am I right?" We realize we can't be right enough to make things happen as we want. Instead we ask, "Whom do I trust?"

The passion to explain leads us along a path that ends badly. According to Isaiah, we end up lying down in torment, wracked by unanswerable questions: Why didn't this work? What could I have done differently? Why am I so stupid? Why did I ever listen to that expert? How can I possibly climb out of this hole? It's so deep—and dark.

But when the passion to be right is mortified, a new one arises: a longing to trust God. And that urge takes us on a sometimes bumpy and steep path that winds through some very dark nights but eventually brings us to green pastures. There we lie down, in rest. And that's a guarantee.

CHAPTER 12

Two More Urges to Be Killed

C ity builders fail to connect because they are more interested in proving their adequacy. Fire lighters work harder at being right than at giving what they have. Two more urges that need to be killed are suggested by the metaphors of wall whitewashing and well digging.

WALL WHITEWASHING: A COMMITMENT TO SAFETY

The Metaphor

One of the most unsettling elements of living in this world is its uncertainty. We're never entirely sure what's about to happen. Crystal balls aren't reliable, and the only source that always knows won't tell.

My wife and I just spent two hours chatting with a woman whose husband may die tomorrow, or a year from now. His diagnosis of brain cancer came a decade ago. I've been recently waking up every morning with a strange headache. Should I get a brain scan? To worry whether every new pain means a serious illness is hypochondriasis. To be certain I'm fine is pretense. We just don't know what lies ahead.

Parents of adult children used to tell me that their burdens didn't end at graduation or when their children married well or after a good job came along. I thought they were overstating it a bit. Now I don't. Even though our two sons are doing well—happily married, responsibly working, involved in good churches—we simply do not know what tomorrow will bring for them, for us, for anyone.

People hate uncertainty. We're scared to death over what our unpredictable God might allow or not prevent (however that works). He promises to withhold nothing good, to bless us with spiritual blessings, and to weave whatever happens into a good plan.

But at times it's all so hard to believe. What's the point of *this,* we ask? A six-year-old asthmatic child fighting to breathe, a cancer-filled husband lingering in pain, a friend's betrayal that you never saw coming, a job loss just when the first kid goes off to college. It just doesn't make sense.

There must be a way to live, we think, that at least lowers the probability of bad things happening. Especially those bad things we fear the most. I could handle *this* Lord but not *that.* Surely you wouldn't permit *that* to happen.

The Israelites in Isaiah's day must have been stirred by similar concerns when they instructed their spiritual leaders: "Tell us pleasant things, prophesy illusions. . . . Stop confronting us with the Holy One of Israel" (Isa. 30:10–11). Seeing God as he really is does not always inspire immediate comfort. He lets bad things happen to good people, people like us who, though depraved, are surely good enough to be spared really bad things. We want protection, whether vitamins to prevent cancer, insurance to prevent bankruptcy, or tips to prevent family disaster. Tell us that good things are on the horizon, and not just the horizon of heaven. That's too far away. We want protection from bad things now.

Israel's prophets complied with the people's wishes, a pattern not uncommon today. They prophesied "out of their own imagination" and declared peace when there was no peace (Ezek. 13:3, 10). But then they went a step further.

To protect themselves from enemy raids, the townspeople had built walls around their cities, walls that in fact were flimsy but walls the Israelites desperately wanted to believe would keep them safe. The leaders should have said, "Your walls will not keep you safe. They are flimsy. Only God can be trusted. Do not trust in what you can make, but only in Almighty God."

Instead, they painted the walls with whitewash to make them look sturdier. They provided false comfort, false hope, a false sense of protection. "Now," the people thought, "surely nothing bad can happen. Our spiritual leaders have helped us to feel safe."

Listen to God's response:

> "Tell those who cover it [the wall] with whitewash that it is going
> to fall.... I will tear down the wall you have covered with whitewash
> and will level it to the ground." (Ezek. 13:11, 14)

God would not permit the work of the wall whitewashers to stand.

The Meaning of the Metaphor

God does not honor our passion for safety, at least not on our terms.
He values our trust, even as he refuses to guarantee our safety from difficulty and disaster. The line from the familiar hymn, "I know not what the
future holds but I know who holds the future," expresses more than warm
sentiment; it's what God thinks our attitude should be.

But it's tough. When we hear of bad things happening to someone, we
reflexively throw whitewash on whatever walls we think might protect us
from a similar tragedy. Friends in my church just lost their twenty-five-
year-old son to a rock-climbing accident, a month before he was to graduate from the Air Force Academy. We have two boys, twenty-six and
twenty-eight at the time of this writing. I hurt for my friends, but when I
heard of their loss, I had to push back the terror that it could happen in
our family.

A close friend's college-aged son recently flipped a buddy over his head
while rehearsing a skit. It was all good fun, the kind of thing that happens
a thousand times a year on college campuses where guys good-naturedly
wrestle or try gymnastic stunts or prepare skits for parties.

But this time the young man landed on his neck and is now paralyzed
from the chest down.

When I heard what happened, I longed to connect with my friend. I
love the man. I wanted to connect with the paralyzed student. I wanted to
say, "We don't know what the doctors can accomplish. But you will come
to know God as few people ever do. We will support you on your journey."
I wanted to connect with my friend's son, the young man who flipped his
buddy, as he repeats the "what if . . ." question over and over to himself.

All that was there. But something else was too. As I prayed for the
many folks affected by this accident (and continue to pray), and as I

reflected on the hardships involved, I could hear a nagging little whisper, "How can I make sure this will never happen to one of my sons?"

A natural reaction? Of course; a natural reaction of the flesh. To long for my family's safety is, of course, legitimate and a legitimate reason for prayer. To do all that I can to prevent tragedies from occurring is reasonable and prudent. Nothing wrong there. But to quietly *demand* that I find some way to protect my family from bad things and to then trust in the protection I provide is wall whitewashing.

Wall whitewashers focus on a two-part question: Am I safe? And if I'm not, what can I do to guarantee my safety? They connect, falsely, with people who provide the apparent means of protecting their lives from whatever they fear. Christian communities sometimes bond together by splashing whitewash on each other's walls, by agreeing that certain actions and attitudes have persuaded God to preserve them from disaster.

Wall whitewashers hate uncertainty more than they trust God. They demand protection and provide it for themselves when God doesn't. The effect of their commitment to safety is that their souls never find rest in Christ. And their desire to connect with others is thwarted. Their priority concern for their own safety acts as a valve, closing off the outflow of loving energy.

So God, in his relentless determination to mold us into a connecting community that centers on Christ, goes to work. Sometimes he allows us to experience the disaster we thought could never happen.

My brother's death in a plane crash in 1991 rocked my faith, mostly by exposing that I was trusting in whitewashed walls more than in my Father's heart. This couldn't happen to our family. Bill was walking with the Lord, a godly man, making an impact as a Christian counselor, a good husband, father, son, and brother. So many things were going right in our family. Surely we were safe from *that* level of disaster.

But on Sunday morning, March 3, 1991, my flimsy whitewashed walls were suddenly torn down.

Being an inveterate wall whitewasher, I took some comfort in other things going well. My marriage was solid. Our sons were doing well. My ministry was thriving. And I had a pretty good handle on what I believed about counseling and my contribution to the kingdom.

Then came the shifts in my thinking about counseling that prompted this book. Some were small, some not so small; but they headed me in a new direction. I've heard it variously described as the product of my getting older and perhaps a little tired, of undealt-with issues in my deceitful heart that need repentance, of thinking that just isn't as sharp as it used to be, of a pioneering courage that is leading in wonderful directions, of the Holy Spirit speaking through me.

Which is it? What's behind my new direction? Where am I heading? Where will it all lead? I'm not entirely sure. Nothing has ever felt clearer to me than what I'm now teaching, but I can't know for *certain* where it's coming from or where it's going. And, some of the time, I don't like that one bit. I remind myself that I've consulted with lots of good minds, that I've faced the criticism as honestly as I know how, that my conviction deepens as I continue to study Scripture and pray.

Drawing strength from these reminders is legitimate. But if I depend on these good things to protect me from future ministry difficulties (which I properly don't want to happen) then I'm a wall whitewasher. Wall whitewashers cannot welcome tribulations as friends. Difficulties that we thought would never happen become enemies. Character isn't the goal of a wall whitewasher. Safety is.

But God does not honor that passion. He sometimes allows seasons of unexplained and entirely unreasonable difficulties to come along like hailstorms to knock down our walls. It's then that we're confronted with a choice: Will we build another wall and cover it with paint? Will we yield to our urge for safety and make it a priority? *Or* will we resist that urge and instead do what the Spirit leads us to do, knowing we will be protected only from that which interferes with God's purposes? When prayer does not prevent plane crashes, will we stop praying because prayer didn't work? Or will we keep on praying because it connects us with God and releases our good hearts to bless others?

The passion for safety, when it becomes our final line of defense against disaster, is an urge to be killed. It needs to die. Difficulties with no clear point or cause may be required to help us mortify the urge, to throw it aside as a controlling motive in our lives. Only as that urge is killed every time it appears will we connect as we could.

WELL DIGGING: A COMMITMENT TO SATISFACTION

The Metaphor

In a remarkable passage, God calls the heavens to come look at what his people are doing. The triune God who created humans to share in the fun of his community is (can we say it?) exasperated. "Can you believe it?" he seems to be saying. "They're all thirsty yet they walk right by the water I provide. Then they grab a shovel to go dig their own wells. It makes no sense.

"And the wells they dig spring leaks every time. They get a mouthful of water, then it's gone. Then they go dig another one. You'd think they would return to the living water I freely provide that's available in abundance. But they insist on drinking from their own wells. It is simply unbelievable. It's absolute foolishness." (See Jeremiah 2:13–14.)

Well digging highlights our urge for immediate satisfaction on demand and on terms we control. It's another urge to be killed.

The Meaning of the Metaphor

I just watched the movie *Mr. Holland's Opus* on video. My son Ken has been pressing me for some time to see it, so, as a break from writing about well digging, I watched it. Naturally, with my mind full of thoughts about connecting, I assumed the story was written to illustrate what I intended to say in this chapter.

At one point in the movie, music teacher Glen Holland drives a student-driver car (with two students in it) like a madman to reach the hospital where his wife has just given birth. The joy of that moment—holding your firstborn child and kissing the woman who carried and delivered the fruit of your union—is wonderfully portrayed. I thought about the birth of our two sons and the woman who let me join with her to help create them.

Within a year the Hollands discover their son, Cole, is deaf. Their joy turns to grief, a grief especially hard for the music-loving father to handle. He will never be able to connect with his son with what is so close to the center of his soul.

He responds poorly. Mr. Holland disconnects from Cole, assuming there is no deeper level at which they can meet.

For me, the most touching moment in the movie comes when Mr. Holland recognizes in Cole, perhaps now sixteen, a passion for life that exists beneath his hearing loss. It finally dawns on Mr. Holland that Cole longs to be a part of his father's life, and could be, through a medium far richer than music, a medium that deafness can't block.

During a concert, Mr. Holland, composer, director, pianist, but not vocalist, puts down his baton, steps to the microphone, and announces that he wants to sing a song and dedicate it to his son. He then sings (and signs) "My Beautiful Child" by John Lennon. Cole reads the signing and reads his father's lips. Something comes out of the father that pours into the son, leaving Mr. Holland trembling with joy and Cole glowing with received love.

Connecting occurs. Mr. Holland's dreams of *lesser* connection have died, and he enters into the joy of something far greater.

God offers us a richer joy than anything else provides, the joy of listening to him sing to us with sheer delight in spite of all our deficiencies and then singing to another with the same passion.

But our unnecessary yet inevitable struggles with adequacy, confidence, and safety create so much noise that we don't hear the music. And that leaves us empty in the place within us that longs to be in a relationship of mutual delight.

Our emptiness becomes a problem. We experience it as soul pain, a profoundly empty space that demands to be filled.[1] But because we don't listen to the Lord's music, because we don't drink from his well, we settle for lesser satisfaction, for anything that relieves the infernal ache within.

We want pleasure that we can control to fill us with joy. But it can't be done. It won't happen. Still we try, sometimes with obvious things like pornography, overeating, and money; other times with less obvious things like prestige, competence, or power. We demand a pleasurable feeling that eliminates the ache. But that won't come till heaven. Even when we hear Christ singing, we're still aware of loved ones who have shut their ears to his music, of a friend dying of cancer, of relationships that just don't work. Until heaven, the joy of the Lord coexists with sadness—the richer the joy, the deeper the sadness, an experience that keeps us focused on Christ and what's ahead.

However, when our hope wavers, when sadness gets the upper hand, sadness changes into bitterness. We learn to hate whatever emptiness we feel and fear that it will continue forever, and worsen.

That's the dynamic of a well digger. Well diggers are ruled by an urge to feel good now, completely, to generate an internal experience of well-being that has no sadness involved. Their question becomes, "Am I fulfilled?" That's all that matters.

Well diggers evaluate their relationships, their careers, their bank accounts, their day-to-day activities with one criterion: Do these things satisfy me? And they find themselves regularly answering no. Our souls were built for a satisfaction that only heaven can provide. Then the ache will finally be gone.

As the ache continues to be felt beneath the available pleasures, two things happen. First, we begin demanding more satisfaction and living to get it. Whatever provides even a brief experience of ache-free happiness becomes irresistible. The urge to feel now what we will only feel in heaven dominates us; we change jobs, leave spouses, try new churches, live for bigger ministries, eat too much, indulge increasingly perverted sexual urges, do whatever gives momentary satisfaction.

Second, we assume responsibility to arrange for the pleasures we want. We dig our own wells. It feels good to know that satisfaction is available on demand. We don't like being at the mercy of an unpredictable God.

The urge for satisfaction then flourishes. It consumes us. It determines every choice we make.

Then God goes to work to help us mortify this passion of the flesh. He often helps well diggers learn to hate their well digging by smacking them in the face with the damage their pursuit of pleasure causes others. Recognition of that damage disturbs Christians' new hearts.

A friend of mine became severely depressed when his ministry ended. He was forced to engage in menial work just to make ends meet. His abilities were no longer respected and used as they had been: *The city builder had been taken to the desert.* He had no idea how to plan the next stage of his life: *The fire lighter was plunged into darkness.* He couldn't understand why things fell apart after so many years of faithful and fruitful service: *The wall whitewasher experienced difficulties he thought he'd never encounter.* He felt inadequate, confused, and unsafe, respectively those things that city builders, fire lighters, and wall whitewashers hate and fear the most.

Needless to say, the pain was intense. One evening after another day of discouraging work, on a whim he stopped by an adult bookstore, something he'd never done before, and rented a pornographic video. As he watched it later that same night, all his troubles were for one wonderful hour completely forgotten. It was his first experience of pain-free living in years.

Over the next several weeks, he rented and watched a dozen videos, always after his wife had gone to bed. Late one night, while he was viewing his twelfth movie, she got out of bed, walked into the family room, and found him glued to the images on the screen, masturbating.

Of course she had known what was going on and had many times railed on him, coldly ignored him, and threatened separation. This time she wept. She felt overcome by the pain in her heart and by the moral tragedy unfolding before her. She simply stood there and cried, for maybe five minutes, then turned, and without a word went back to bed.

His shame was acute. But even more distressing was his realization of how badly he was damaging his wife. She felt abandoned, unwanted, and cheap. He knew it. And as that terrible reality slapped him in the face, a longing was aroused within him to bless his wife, a desire that felt stronger than ever before. In one moment of the Spirit's convicting work, he saw that the pleasures of illicit sex were denying him the satisfaction he really wanted, the joy of bringing a smile to the face of his wife.

And, just as important, he realized that the urge for immediate satisfaction was not central to his being, that it was an enemy already defeated that did not need to control him. Something more fundamental than "sex addict" defined him. He was a *Christian,* with sexual struggles.

With the help of two friends with whom he shared these struggles, he made no provision for further illicit satisfaction, he got rid of the magazine collection he had hidden, and he began nourishing his spirit with prayer, time in the Word, and fellowship with his two buddies.

That man is now drinking from the living water. He has thrown away his shovel, he is putting the demand for satisfaction to death, he occasionally still wrestles with strong temptation (slipped a few times), and he is aggressively loving his wife.

The urge to feel completely good now, to be able to arrange for intense satisfaction whenever we want it, to depend on no one who might refuse to cooperate: That's an urge to be killed. It comes out of our flesh and must die. Sometimes it takes facing the damage we do to others when we indulge that urge to help us put it to death.

We've been looking at the obstacles to connecting. In the next chapter I explore how connecting with others can help us overcome those obstacles and what overcoming them entails.

CHAPTER 13

Connecting in the Heat of Battle

It is hard to be seen at your worst. Perhaps that's why our deepest tears are often shed alone. We're afraid friends will tire of our struggles, so we keep them to ourselves, especially the ugly ones that we can't quite manage to put behind us.

But tears without an audience, without someone to hear and care, leave the wounds unhealed. When someone listens to our groanings and stays there, we feel something change inside us. Despair seems less necessary; hope begins to stir where before there was only pain.

Remember my friend who sat with me while I cried. An hour later, he turned to me with reddened eyes and said, "My stomach literally hurts over how much pain you're feeling." He heard me and cared.

It was a moment of connection. Something powerful poured out of his soul toward something alive and good in mine, and I was strengthened. How did he learn to do that? Had he practiced a technique? Attended a seminar on "connection skills"? Or, has he allowed suffering to tear down a few obstacles getting in the way of releasing the good God has already placed within him?

His words were not the "right" ones. Don't jot them down and recite them the next time your friend falls apart. They simply poured out of a heart that, at that moment, was ruled by the energy of Christ. I caught a glimpse of the Father that day. With a little more conviction, I believed he cared too.

We must face the hard truth that no one loves well who hasn't suffered.

Those bad urges that corrupt our efforts to love die only in the midst of trials, such as desert experiences, confusing darkness, seemingly pointless difficulties, and admitted damage that our selfishness has caused.

When others unburden themselves, the listeners usually feel inadequate. We don't know what to say. We think something deeper is going on that we can't see and wouldn't know how to handle if we did. So we offer bland advice, or offer to pray, or maybe take a stab at empathy ("Sounds like you're really scared"), or interpretation ("Do you think your fear of rejection has something to do with your father abandoning you when you were a little girl?"). Or we mutter a few biblical phrases about God or heaven, and hope they do some good. Or we refer.

Training is required, we assume, to say really helpful words. But maybe our problem is not lack of training. *Maybe the problem is the feeling of inadequacy itself.* That feeling, I suggest, often has more to do with wanting to be adequate than with legitimate inadequacy. A friend who has not been to dental school is inadequate to repair your cracked tooth. That's legitimate inadequacy. But a friend who doesn't release the good that God has placed within when you share your burdens may be struggling more with the fruit of city building than with a real lack.

City building is behind most of the felt inadequacy that keeps people from connecting in the body of Christ. If we depend on internal competency to help a hurting friend, we will usually feel inadequate. (Who do we think is competent? And how do we think they got that way?) But if we look to see what is stirring within our redeemed hearts as we engage with a troubled friend, we may find something powerful to release. The bad passion of city building (demand for adequacy) must die if the good passion of kingdom building (longing to give) is to be released.

A city builder's bad urges, with the crippling sense of inadequacy they generate, die best in the desert. My friend has spent time in the desert, he has and does wrestle with terrible feelings of worthlessness, and he has sometimes battled alone, with no audience for his tears but God. Those battles had a lot to do with releasing Christ's energy toward me that day.

Fire lighters would greet my tears with frantic mental activity, wanting to feel confident in a good plan for responding to my tears. They might enroll in counselor training courses to better handle a similar situation next time. Fire lighters are the counseling students who tell their supervisors, "OK, tell me what to do when this happens!"

Merely instructing fire lighters to demand fewer strategies and to trust their hearts has little effect. That advice doesn't sound like a good plan. "Trust my heart? How can I do that and end up knowing exactly what's the best way to help?" Only darkness deep enough to make plans impossible to devise will make the idea of trust attractive.

My friend trained under me in counseling. But when I cried he didn't mentally thumb through his lecture notes to decide how best to handle me. He has spent time in the darkness where he had no idea what to do next in critical situations. The darkness has taught him a little of what it means to trust the Spirit of Christ within him.

Suppose I had presented my tears to a wall whitewasher. A wall whitewasher would feel the pressure to make things better, or at least make them *look* better, as quickly as possible. Maybe prayer would do the job; perhaps strong rebuke is called for; warm words and a big hug worked well with someone else who was hurting last month; it's worth another try.

Real engagement is out of the question. It doesn't even occur to a wall whitewasher: too risky. A flimsy wall designed to keep out trouble is quickly built and covered with whitewash. A chance to connect is missed. But that's acceptable: The goal was reached. Everyone feels a little better, and no big risks were taken.

My friend was committed to a different goal. He longed to touch me, to give me whatever was in him that reflected Christ. That goal has become more real in his life during times of facing difficulties he couldn't avoid. Those seasons ruined his hopes for safety; higher hopes then emerged.

When we don't connect, we feel empty. We were designed to connect by a connecting God. Anything less leaves us with an awful ache that we mightily wish wasn't there. The ache can be so bad that whatever relieves it, even for a moment, can seem good. The worst crimes—things like rape, cheating, and violence—can feel justified because, for one wonderful minute, the ache is gone. "Lesser" crimes like sarcasm, indifference, and patronizing are even easier to justify. They feel so good. The seasonal pleasures of sin do eliminate that terrible ache, not for long, perhaps, but nothing else seems to relieve it at all.

That's how well diggers think. Had my friend been a well digger, he would have scurried about to find some way to feel satisfaction as he tried to comfort his weeping friend. He might have envisioned himself as a hero, rescuing this public Christian from trials only he had seen. Or he might have tried the more usual route of indulging private sexual fantasies while he looked at me with concern.

But that's not what happened. He struggled for me with the energy of Christ, partly, I believe, because a few months earlier he faced how badly he had failed me. Realizing the impact of his selfishness made him hate that selfishness—because he loves me—and opened him up to the far better passions within him. By the grace of God, he is a *good* man. He is no longer a bad man. That change took place when he became a Christian. And he discovered more of the goodness within him by seeing the wounds his badness had inflicted.

My friend spends time feeling crushed by the damage he is capable of doing. And that awareness releases his urge to bless.

The passions of our independent nature get in the way of connecting. They need to die. And we are called to participate in the execution, to load the gun and pull the trigger.

At this point in our discussion, two remaining questions need brief attention. First, how does connecting help us kill our bad urges? And second, exactly what does it mean to mortify, to put to death, our bad passions? Why does the Bible speak of killing them? Are we supposed to eliminate those urges so they never plague us again? If not, aren't we really talking about merely resisting them and not killing them at all?

HOW DOES CONNECTING HELP?

It is not the job of community to change people. Only the Spirit can do that. And he is the one responsible to lead people into the desert or deepen their darkness or to introduce unexplained difficulties into their lives or convince them of the damage their selfishness has caused. He sometimes uses us as instruments in bringing those things about, but responsibility for creating redemptive pain is a job that belongs in hands more tender than ours. We may sometimes rebuke and provide disruptive feedback (we must always do it reluctantly), but we must never insist that our disruption accomplish a deep spiritual work. We must never demand a response to our intervention, but rather we should pray for one.

When we do require that our involvement generate an effect, we usurp the Holy Spirit's role and usually find ourselves in the middle of a power struggle. The central calling of community is to connect, not to disrupt, to release something powerful from within one person into the life of another that calls forth the goodness in another's heart. And the work of God's Spirit in helping us overcome the obstacles to connecting (wrong agendas like adequacy, confidence, safety, and satisfaction) provides rich opportunities for uniquely powerful connecting. Let me explain.

When times are hard, we need each other most. When the Spirit leads a city builder to the desert, the pain of inadequacy is keenly felt. A friend wrote me a long letter; every page was stained with tears. "No one is following me," he said, and it was causing him to wonder if there was anything in him worth following. "It's as though I am consumed with being this incredibly powerful person who people listen to all the time."

My friend is in the desert. His city-building demands are becoming clearer to him, and the pain when those demands aren't met is growing more acute. For years he has struggled to prove his adequacy, partly in response to an upbringing that provided little affirmation. In many ways, he has done well. He is a capable, talented, highly intelligent man. But he has not yet found rest.

Because God loves him and wants him to die to his requirement of adequacy, God's Spirit is taking him on a long walk through hot sand without shoes. He is in a situation where he is not adequate, where his resources are not enough to make life work. Time in the desert is designed to encourage him to give up the goal of personal adequacy and devote his talents to building God's kingdom. Only in the desert can we recognize that we have been building our own city (even though the work we have been doing may have all the trappings of ministry).

And then, when we are broken by that realization and repent, the possibility of a new agenda becomes inviting. We begin to sense what it could mean to live by the Spirit.

Picture the process this way:

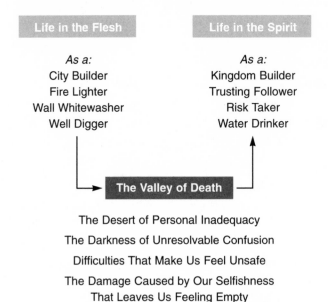

Life in the Flesh

As a:
City Builder
Fire Lighter
Wall Whitewasher
Well Digger

Life in the Spirit

As a:
Kingdom Builder
Trusting Follower
Risk Taker
Water Drinker

The Valley of Death

The Desert of Personal Inadequacy
The Darkness of Unresolvable Confusion
Difficulties That Make Us Feel Unsafe
The Damage Caused by Our Selfishness
That Leaves Us Feeling Empty

My friend is in the desert. And that presents me with an opportunity. If I can see goodness in him, if I believe the Spirit is up to something wonderful in his life, then I can search my heart to see what's there that could be poured into his to touch the goodness I know is there. However I might express it, the message I want to convey, the message that is in me is, "I believe in you."

Suppose my friend felt more confused than inadequate. Suppose the Spirit was leading him into a dark valley where he couldn't see a lighted path ahead, perhaps questions about how bills were to be paid or how best to respond to an unmarried pregnant daughter. Rather than merely agreeing that the situation is confusing or giving advice, I could again search my heart to find my deepest response, the reaction that flows out of my new heart. To a friend confused by darkness, I might want to say, "I know you long to trust God. I will never tire of your struggle to do so."

When the valley has more to do with unexplained difficulties, when God is pelting a person's whitewashed walls with hailstones to turn him from safety to courage, his Spirit might stir us to say, "You are a person of courage. I deeply respect that." Perhaps those words would connect with a redeemed wall whitewasher who needs to give up the illusion of protection and move forward with responsible risk taking. That's what he *wants* to do. I know that because the Spirit of God is moving in his regenerate heart to live by God's design.

And finally, when we are broken by the harm our sin has caused another, no words are sweeter than, "I forgive you." The Spirit of God sees something beautiful beneath the ugliness. He knows it's in us because he put it there. And when he stirs someone else to see it, too, it frees that person to forgive the offense in hopes of releasing what is good.

Perhaps a simply organized summary of all these points will help us keep them in mind.

Metaphor #1: City Building

Core Agenda:	I will make my life work through resources I can control.
Preoccupying Question:	"Am I adequate?"
Deep Fear:	Inadequacy
Angry Demand:	"Affirm me!"
Opportunity for False Connection:	Working with people whose mutual competencies enable them to achieve a common goal
Related Urges:	Jealousy Enjoyment of another's misfortune Dependence on compliments Hypersensitivity to criticism
God's Strategy for Helping:	Time in the desert
The Message of Connection:	"I believe in you."
New Question:	"What can I give?"

Metaphor #2: Fire Lighting

Core Agenda:	I will find a plan that I know will work.

Preoccupying Question:	"Am I right?"
Deep Fear:	Confusion
Angry Demand:	"Agree with me." "Tell me what will work."
Opportunity for False Connection:	Finding people who agree with us and dogmatically asserting the wisdom of our understanding while judging others who see things differently
Related Urges:	Desire to divide Eagerness to criticize Love of argument Condescending spirit
God's Strategy for Helping:	Deepening the darkness
The Message of Connection:	"You long to trust him."
New Question:	"Whom do I trust?"

Metaphor #3: Wall Whitewashing

Core Agenda:	I will protect myself against the difficulties of life; that is my priority.
Preoccupying Question:	"Am I safe?"
Deep Fear:	Disaster
Angry Demand:	"Align with me." (Help me protect myself.)
Opportunity for False Connection:	Living in community with folks who emphasize only the blessings of life and attribute those blessings to something they've done
Related Urges:	Obsessive tendencies Shallow spirituality Disciplined habits Unadventurous

God's Strategy for Helping:	Introducing difficulties that cannot be protected against
The Message of Connection:	"I see courage in you."
New Question:	"Am I in good enough hands to aggressively move into life?"

Metaphor #4: Well Digging

Core Agenda:	I want to feel good when I want to and in a way that eliminates all pain, if only for a moment.
Preoccupying Question:	"Am I fulfilled?"
Deep Fear:	Emptiness
Angry Demand:	Acquiescence: "Cooperate with my efforts to feel good and don't judge me."
Opportunity for False Connection:	Associating with superficial people who have no higher goal than enjoying life
Related Urges:	Impatience
	Insensitivity
	Indulgence
	Greed
God's Strategy for Helping:	Exposing the damage in others that selfishness can cause
The Message of Connection:	"You're forgiven."
New Question:	"How can I bless?"

What Does It Mean to Kill Our Urges?

Bad urges exist within us. Not many question that. And we are to resist them. No Christian argues otherwise.

But we're told to do more than resist them. We're to put them to death. And yet we would all confess that bad urges are still alive within us; we continue to feel their force. Does that mean we haven't killed them? Or does putting them to death indicate something other than eliminating them?

Let me suggest three things that mortifying the flesh does not mean.

1. *It does not mean merely resisting them.* Certainly it includes resistance (we are to say no to worldly desires, Titus 2:12), but it involves something more. Otherwise, we are back to a do-what's-right approach, quaking at the foot of Mt. Sinai while the law tells us what to do.

2. *It does not mean eliminating them so their pull is never felt again.* Psychotherapy sometimes holds out that hope. Cure the underlying psychological disorder and, just like when a doctor cures pneumonia, the symptoms disappear. No more troubling passions. But urges of the flesh do not disappear when psychological problems are treated.

3. *It does not mean scrutinizing every impending choice for underlying bad urges and, if we find them, choosing other directions.* A friend was part of a group counseling experience that worked to expose ugly motives beneath every behavior. Each member "shared" the negative impact they felt from every other member's style of relating. My friend left the group shattered, convinced there was nothing in her but bad urges. She became afraid to say much of anything to people for fear she would damage someone else. Predictably, she lost all joy and freedom. What her counseling group did is not what the Bible means by mortifying the flesh.

Paul tells us that our *old self* was crucified with Christ so that "we should no longer be slaves to sin" (Rom. 6:6). Something has already been killed by Christ—we had no part in it—but now we are free to treat as dead what he has already destroyed.

The strict meaning of the word old (in old self) is "worn out," or "wornness." It signifies something that has outlived its usefulness and is no longer to be desired. When Paul says that our old self has been crucified, he uses a word for crucified that means thoroughly destroyed.

What he is saying is this: The way we approached life before we met Christ is utterly useless, and the death of Christ has treated it as useless and has removed it from its former position of authority in our lives. Not only are our sins (the product of that old way of living) forgiven, but our sin nature has also been supplanted by something better and more powerful.

The old nature continues to exist as a source of bad urges, but it has been exposed as a power that has no value in giving us life. It has been dethroned as the only leader to which we could turn to find the wholeness we desire. A new leader has entered our lives, a leader we are now free to serve.

All that has been done for us. But it is now our job to "count [our]selves dead to sin" (Rom. 6:11), to clearly see that the flesh (our demand that we find adequacy, confidence, safety, and satisfaction without giving up our independence) is a worn-out, useless approach to life. It just doesn't work, even though it seems to for a while. It leads to misery, inevitably, in every case.

But we still have trouble seeing it that way. So God takes us to the desert where our claim to adequacy is proven false; he places us in darkness where our hopes for confidence in clear strategies are dashed; he introduces difficulties into our lives that we thought we had protected ourselves against; and he forcefully opens our eyes to how much our indulgent living hurts others, thus spoiling our pleasure in sin. He is demonstrating in our immediate experience that the passions of the flesh do not lead to life, as they promise; they lead to misery, unhappiness, despair, futility.

God's Spirit loves to highlight the beauty of Christ, a beauty that is now in us. Everything he does has this purpose in view. When he sees urges within us that take us away from Christ, he exposes them as dangerous to our spiritual health and useless to our hope for experiencing life.

When we recognize what is already true, that our old self is powerless to control us and that there is no value (and great damage) in letting it do so, then, when we choose to resist bad urges, we are mortifying the flesh. We are killing sinful passions as tyrants in our lives that we think will give us good things.

The Spirit's central concern is to release the life of Christ within us. He never enjoys the pain we feel when we experience the desert or darkness or difficulties or the damage we cause. He is simply clearing out the obstacles to connecting, to living in relationships that provide the same joy the Father, Son, and Spirit have always, except for one Friday afternoon, enjoyed.

But not only must we mortify the flesh in order to connect, we must also vivify the Spirit. What that means is my final topic.

CHAPTER 14

It's Time to Connect

My wife's father died March 10, 1997. He was ninety-one years old. No death leaves those left behind unaffected. It's never easy. Every death is a unique event with its own trail of grieving.

Certainly this is true of a father's death. When that man, the one who was meant to embody the ideals of protection, strength, and advocacy, leaves this world, his passing stirs a bewildering variety of emotions. Individual memories return with a force they couldn't have while he lived. And the big picture, the threads and larger themes that the particular events of his life point to, comes more clearly into focus. Isolated specifics, though still very much alive with the power to warm or chill our hearts, tend to be caught up in a larger whole. Usually.

Sometimes a few terrible memories carry such weight that no better themes are recognized. Occasionally the reverse happens. One or two wonderful bits of history are used to create a positive image that honesty about the rest of the story would shatter.

Most often, specific memories, whether good or bad, still arouse strong feelings, but enduring patterns that define the father's character and reveal his abiding impact are more noticed and pondered. The longing to see oneself as heir to a good legacy is intensified by a father's death.

That longing often creates a difficult tension between what we remember and what we wish we could remember. It takes some work to genuinely appreciate the strengths that blessed us while still facing, without resentment, the weaknesses that caused us pain.

That conflict usually remains underground for about six weeks after the funeral. The immediate force of the shock subsides by then and the thousand details requiring attention have either been handled or a plan to do what needs to be done is in place. The heart then feels the freedom to express its deeper struggles, that are best faced with a community that connects.

Rachael and I are part of a Sunday school class that is becoming an increasingly meaningful community. We're taking seriously the opportunity the gospel presents to connect with one another, to release what is alive and strong within us in a way that stimulates what is good in each other.

Three members of our class have recently experienced the death of a parent. Mary lost her mother and Sandy her father, both to cancer. Rachael watched her dad descend into nearly paralyzing weakness and sometimes bizarre disorientation before he rose up, healthy and alert, in Christ's presence.

The class sponsored an evening we simply called a grief time for each of these women. Along with Al Stirling, the man who carries most of the burden for shepherding our little community, I was involved in planning and leading the evenings for Mary and Sandy.

Rachael's grief time was last week, about six weeks after her father died. I came as her husband with no responsibility other than to be with my wife. Two grandchildren, one of our sons and a nephew who lives locally, attended as well.

Among my many reactions to the evening, I found myself hoping that I would still be a part of this community when one of my parents dies. I want these friends to gather around me as I grieve.

A stronger reaction involved a clear sense that I was in the middle of a healing community, that something powerful was pouring out of our friends into my wife and enlivening the goodness within her. A few Christians connected that evening in a way that only the gospel makes possible.

We gathered at six-thirty, nearly sixty of us responding to Bill and Sandy's initiative to make this evening happen. For half an hour, we sampled, smorgasbord-style, the dozen desserts that lined the kitchen counter. Mary baked a cherry pie; it's Rachael's favorite.

Jeannie brought a special gift. Earlier that week, she had heard Rachael describe the cookie jars her father loved to keep handy, one always filled with animal crackers for him and his fourteen grandchildren and thirteen great-grandchildren to enjoy. When Rachael sorted through his things, the cookie jars she found touched a tender spot. She experienced regret that she hadn't kept one as a memento. At her grief night, Rachael received a glass cookie jar, filled with animal crackers, with a sweet note from Jeannie. It was a moment of connecting; no technical skill was required, just sensitivity and kindness.

Like each of us, Rachael's dad was an imperfect person, a tangle of contradictions, some remarkable strengths and a few infuriating weaknesses. His impact on my wife's soul included rich blessing and deep hurt. He both nourished and damaged her. Rachael came to the evening apprehensive, aware of both her wounds and warmth. She wanted to neither disparage her father nor pedestalize him.

When the pie pans were picked over, the formal part of the evening began, a little after seven. Though never put this way, the community's intention was to encourage Rachael to mortify whatever fleshly responses existed toward her father and to help vivify her spirit, where the life of Christ was present. The group wanted to see her embrace her pain without stirring up resentment, and everyone desired to nourish her confidence in God's goodness in a way that would allow her to connect with what was noble and gracious within her.

Al began with a few words about the value of remembering and then invited Rachael to introduce her dad to the group, first by recalling memories from when she was a little girl. Before she responded, Rachael played a song on her dad's tape recorder that had provided substantial comfort during the past several weeks. She had heard it on Christian radio some months earlier and mentioned how much she liked it to a friend. That friend found the song on tape and gave it to Rachael. "If you could see me now," the song begins and then it assures those of us left behind that if we could see our loved one walking on streets of gold, enjoying life as never before, our grief would be surrounded by joy and the fervent anticipation of soon experiencing the same bliss.

When the song ended, Rachael simply said, "I want the reality that these words express to serve as the context for everything I say about my dad. I am really happy for him."

And then, prompted by Al and others with questions like, "What are some of the hard memories?" "How did your dad change over the years?" "What are you most grateful for?" and "What one image do you want to leave in our minds as we think of your father?" Rachael painted a portrait of her dad for more than an hour. The group learned that her father's father had insisted that each of his children carry black people's shopping lists into grocery stores where they weren't allowed, or face a whipping; and this in the deep south. We learned that Rachael's dad would take long walks after work, pockets spilling over with gospel tracts, asking God to send him to the folks that were ready to hear the good news of Christ. We learned that he was a baseball fanatic and would pay Rachael to stay home while he took his sons to major league games. He preferred well-informed masculine company at athletic contests. Rachael was more interested in the social event than the game.

And we learned some things that were not easy for Rachael to share. But in everything that was said, her dad was honored for the good that was in him, and there was much. God was exalted for the good he achieved through her dad's weaknesses.

The evening ended with a chorus of prayers and two hymns especially meaningful to our family. And then the community surrounded Rachael, offering hugs, words of love, and smiles that expressed their delight in the person that is my wife. The community had seen her heart and they jumped up and down at the sight.

One middle-aged woman told me as we lingered (no one wanted to leave) that she had experienced a healing in her soul as she listened to Rachael share. Her father, who had died some years before, had been a stiff, unapproachable man, the kind that would not invite a daughter to snuggle in his lap. She had not been able to get beyond her bitterness over what he had failed to provide her.

But that evening, something deeper than her anger was aroused. She could see the good that God had wrought through her dad. She felt an urge to honor him, to appreciate him, and to worship God as she remembered everything about him. As she described it, "I felt something in me shift."

The passion to forgive her dad, placed there long ago by the Holy Spirit but lying dormant all that time, grew stronger as the urge to hang on to her grudge was put to death.

A power flowed out of my wife and connected with the goodness in this lady's redeemed heart. The life of Christ in one aroused the life of Christ in another. Self-control resulted, and good urges were released. Another moment of connecting.

The evening, wonderful though it was, did not do all that needed to be done in anybody's heart. The battle continues in all of us. The flesh and the spirit still compete in Rachael's heart, in mine, and in those of the rest of the community of friends that gathered that night. Only the return of Christ will forever end the fight, when goodness will completely push aside badness.

Till then, the calling of community is to connect with people, to help them put to death their bad urges, to exercise self-control over unruly and immoral passions, especially during those seasons in the desert, those long nights of darkness, those surprising encounters with seemingly pointless difficulties, and those humbling moments when we see the damage our selfishness caused someone else.

But our calling is more than to help each other mortify the flesh. We also have the means to stimulate each other to love and good deeds, to identify, nourish, and help release the good urges that are always there beneath the bad. Connecting among Christians helps to vivify our spirits.

As I reflected on the time our community of friends met to be with my wife in her loss, it became clear that at least three elements combined to generate the connection we experienced. First, they *entered the battle* for Rachael's soul. They knew that good and bad urges were jockeying for position within her, and they intentionally sided with the good ones.

Second, they believed that God could strengthen Rachael through her grief. They caught a glimpse of the loveliness that defines her and *developed a vision* of what she might look like as the Spirit deepened that loveliness into an even stronger resemblance to Christ.

Third, they *released the energy of Christ* within them on her behalf. Compassion and love prompted them to come. Whatever else was happening in their hearts that evening, perhaps ugly things like jealousy ("Why didn't I get an evening like this when my loved one died?") or self-pity ("I've got so many problems in my life right now, I just can't get into this evening."), the overwhelming sense was that better things ruled in our community as we related. People found what was good within them in the middle of whatever was bad, and they released it.

The effect of these three elements is to reduce our sense of isolation (someone is battling for us), to motivate us to press on toward the prize (we know we will one day be like Christ), and to give us a taste of something so sweet we can settle for nothing less (we have felt the energy of Christ). Connecting releases something good.

Our friends connected with Rachael that evening. It was a wonderful experience, rare, but wonderful. Connecting could become more common in families and among friends. It could become the overflow of worshiping God together. It could become the appeal of the gospel to a disconnected, fragmented generation.

Connecting in our communities the way God connects within the Trinity could revolutionize our understanding of how to help one another.

I spend the last few chapters in this book thinking about the three activities of connecting in the hope that connecting will become more common in your community—and mine.

CHAPTER 15

Entering the Real Battle

What *is the most important thing* going on inside someone at any given moment? What can we talk about in each other's lives that will lead to the deepest possible connection?

Another way of asking the same question is this: What is the most critical battle being fought in our souls? And what hangs in the balance?

As I pick up my pen to write this chapter, I have just put down the telephone. My physician called to check on my health. Five days ago, early Saturday morning, I was awakened from sleep by severe abdominal pain. My wife called the twenty-four-hour emergency hotline.

Fifteen minutes later, I was experiencing my first ambulance ride. Two paramedics had strapped me to a gurney, loaded me into their traveling hospital, invited Rachael to sit up front, and off we went. While a paramedic poked a hole in the back of my hand to start dripping fluids into my blood, I asked him why all the fuss. His answer: "We've got to know which battle we're fighting. Probably nothing serious, but we've got to be sure."

I didn't think of it then—my mind was on other things—but it later occurred to me: Who has worked that hard to know what battle was going on in my soul?

It's often said that we lose our dignity in hospitals. What is meant, I presume, is that a higher priority is placed on identifying the battle raging in our bodies than on preserving our right to physical privacy. But maybe there is a dignity we ought to lose. Maybe in community we should worry less about *personal* privacy than about knowing the battles we are each fighting so we can join in the fray.

In the rear cabin of that ambulance, the paramedic asked me a hundred questions, listened intently to my answers, gave me a dozen instructions (breathe deeply, hold still, lift your arm, and so on), and kept watching me closely for the entire ride. He wanted to identify the real battle, to know if I was close to losing it, and to determine the best way he could help. I liked that. Losing my dignity was a small price to pay.

Again I wonder: Who has been that concerned about my personal struggles? Do I really have to pay someone to be asked that many questions? And, on the other side of things, whose questions would I be willing to answer if they were asked? Would I say to myself it's my business while politely deflecting their inquiries, thinking perhaps that my personal privacy is too precious to give up?

And if I wanted to share the battles going on in my soul, could I? Do I know what they are? I know how to complain, to tell others what I don't like that is happening inside me, but can I express in words the most significant war I'm waging? Is there a more serious struggle going on than I realize?

Two hours in the emergency room at St. Joseph's hospital resulted in a provisional diagnosis of a kidney stone, later confirmed by ultrasound technology. When the paramedics first wheeled me in, the doctor who met me said something that I liked: "We have more pain medicine than you have pain." Immediately, I felt hope. He had already received the paramedic's report, asked a few questions, and given me a medical once-over.

Once again, looking back, I wonder: What powerful words have been spoken to me when my soul was wracked with pain, words that dispelled the gloom and let me imagine a sunny day? The doctor's words were powerful because he was knowledgeably and imminently engaged in the battle. They weren't words printed on a greeting card and sent by someone who heard I was sick. The one who spoke them saw me writhing on the hospital bed. He saw the tears I was trying to hide. Along with most everyone else in the emergency room, he heard my moans, and he took them seriously. He didn't tell me to get a grip on things. He knew how badly I was hurting and still expressed confidence that the battle could be won.

Has anyone ever actually witnessed the contortions my soul sometimes goes through? Whom do I trust enough to be my confessor, to see up close the blood that spills during my spiritual battles, the cowardly retreats I sometimes take, the fears that occasionally paralyze me? If the answer is no one, then do all the words of encouragement I hear have no more power than the sentimental poetry inside greeting cards? Am I willing to lose my personal privacy so that a few people can speak deeply into a battle they understand?

I've been waiting five days now for the stone to pass. A book arrived today, sent by my friends at Word Publishing who know of my current dilemma. It was Max Lucado's *He Still Moves Stones.* My question is *when?*

The stone uncomfortably lodging in quarters too small to host it well has a longer lease than I'd hoped. While a dozen members of Denver's medical community do what they can to evict it, several dozen members of my spiritual community across the country have joined with me to fight the even more important battle going on in my soul.

What is it? It is the battle to trust God when he doesn't seem trustworthy, to hope in him when complaint seems more justified, to draw near to him when he seems indifferent. In a phrase, the battle is to develop a good relationship with God.

I have the makings of it. He's seen to that. The barriers are down, he's declared his dying love, and he has sparked a desire in me to get close. He tells me that nothing, not kidney stone relief, not children doing well, not financial security, not even intimacy with spouse or friends matters more than knowing him well. And I believe him. Almost.

But it's a battle. I want to know him, but I have other interests as well, other concerns that often seem more pressing. If people want to connect with me, it sometimes works better for them to talk with me about those "more important" matters, which have less to do with the supernatural life within me and more to do with the struggles of living in this world. For example:

- The pain I feel in my heart just won't go away. Prayer seems dull; the Bible doesn't meaningfully speak to it; most of my friends don't seem to really care.

- I'm afraid to be really known. I've managed to get along pretty well by wearing masks. If I took them off, I fear I'd be a burden to people, a weight no one would want to bear.

- Life isn't working out exactly as I'd planned. A few big dreams have shattered, and I'm a little wary of coming up with new ones. I couldn't tolerate more disappointment—it resurrects too many questions that I've never really resolved, questions mostly about my value, my sense of adequacy, and whether I'll ever feel really good.

There are other things to hear that belong to an entirely different category, things that more directly bear on the quality of my relationship with God. But to hear them, you must listen well. For example:

- I struggle to believe that I can trust my pain to God and live for something more than relief.

- I long to give what I have to others, to be known by them for their sakes, and to believe that my fear of rejection would be overcome by the blessing of giving.

- I want to surrender my will to God's agenda and pursue whatever direction he leads, regardless of the personal risk involved.

Which battle is more real, the one to preserve my life (reflected in the first list of concerns) or the one to trust Christ with it (reflected in the second list)? Which battle do you more naturally want to enter? If you enter the latter one, will you simply pass out a few Band-Aids and say a prayer, or will you jump into the foxhole and fight along with me?

Passing out Band-Aids takes less time. But when you do that, I begin to think that my spiritual battle isn't such a big one after all. If Band-Aids are all that's needed, maybe the fight is a mild skirmish where only surface wounds are inflicted. Perhaps the real battle (and I know there's a real one going on somewhere) involves my struggle to feel better, to believe in myself, to overcome my self-doubt, that first category of concerns. An entire industry has emerged that offers intensive surgery for the wounds inflicted by that battle.

In our therapeutic culture, we worry endlessly over the impact that dysfunctional families and traumatic events have had on our lives. We focus on our insecurities, our painful memories, and our troubling emotions. Relationship with God is sometimes just one more weapon in the Christian therapist's arsenal that might help us win the battle to find ourselves.

Notice what has happened. The church community tells us that our relationship with God matters most and that its resources are committed to helping us make it better. But the depths of the battle to develop that relationship are rarely defined and entered. They are talked about, but then Band-Aids are offered to cover the cuts we sustain as we fight and a few vitamins are prescribed to keep us strong: Read your Bible, pray more, and don't miss church.[1]

Spiritual leaders in the Old Testament set the pattern. We're told that they dressed the wound of God's people "as though it were not serious. 'Peace, peace,' they say when there is no peace" (Jer. 6:14). Spiritual Band-Aids.

We conclude that the real battle is elsewhere. Psychological stress, emotional scars, sexual confusion, and self-rejection are some of the fronts where the important fight is being fought, or so we think. As the counseling community sends its ambulances to the front lines to deal with the wounds sustained in this battle, the church community breathes a sigh of relief that it can get on with the task of superficially treating spiritual wounds.

As a culture, we have come to regard lesser battles as primary. C. S. Lewis once pointed out that when legitimate but secondary pleasures (like sex) are treated as primary, we eventually enjoy neither. It is equally true that when secondary battles are seen as primary, we lose both.

We have elevated psychological and personal problems to a position of top priority and, in so doing, have relegated the battle to relate well with God to secondary status, important in its own right and sometimes useful in the fight against our personal struggles, but certainly not our most vital and immediately pressing concern.

But that is exactly backward. Had my physician cleared out a potentially dangerous wax buildup in my ears while I writhed in agony from a kidney stone, I would have objected. And yet we accept it when our churches treat our spiritual kidney stone (a deficient relationship with God) with aspirin and then tell us that the pain we still feel is the product of too much ear wax. So off we trot to therapeutic specialists who are skilled at probing our inner ear and removing whatever shouldn't be there. Meanwhile that kidney stone refuses to pass. Our relationship with God stagnates while we assume the solution involves more therapy.

It's time for the church to enter the real battle going on in our souls. Many are already engaged. Here and there, priorities are shifting from providing an inspirational Sunday morning service to leading the people of God in true worship, from offering a smorgasbord of programs that keep everyone happily involved to entering the struggles people are having in their longing to know God well.

The community of God has no higher calling than to seize the opportunity to experience God. Our fiercest battles are fought when we seek with all our heart to *trust* God so fully that we see every misfortune as something he permits and wants to use, to *know* him so richly that we turn to no one and nothing else to experience what our souls long to enjoy, to *love* him so completely and with such consuming passion that we hate anything that comes between us and eagerly give it up.

That's a battle I cannot win alone. I need a community that is waging the same war and will include me in the fight. I need a community that will enter my battle and help me recognize what it is so I don't spend my life fighting lesser ones—which is my tendency.

I tend to evaluate every troubling emotion I feel. Where did it come from? What purpose is it serving? How can I change it? Those are the kind of battles that people take to therapists.

But the bigger battle involves my relationship with God. Do I trust him to continue working in my life even when I am plagued by crippling emotions? Do I know him well enough to turn to him for comfort rather than demand relief from my pain through whatever means are available? Do I love him so deeply that I welcome additional suffering that might draw my soul closer to him? Will I pay *any* price to know him well?

The core battle in everyone's life is to relate well to God, to worship him, enjoy him, experience his presence, hear his voice, trust him in everything, always call him good, obey every command (even the hard ones), and hope in him when he seems to disappear. That's the battle the community of God is called to enter in each other's lives.

When we see that battle as the most important one, it changes our approach to dealing with the lesser but still difficult skirmishes in our life: handling our kids, recovering from divorce, dealing with traumatic memories, coping with loneliness and discouragement.

Imagine what would happen if parents were *less* concerned about keeping their kids off drugs and *more* concerned with entering their children's battles to know God. What would it be like if pastors worried *less* about whether their people were having affairs and *more* about whether they worshiped? Picture a relationship between friends that dealt *less* with their financial and romantic problems and *more* with whether they were experiencing God. The results, I suspect, would likely include fewer kids on drugs, fewer affairs, and fewer nervous break-downs and failed marriages. Connecting begins when we enter into someone else's battle to experience God with the empathy of a fellow struggler and the faith to know it can happen. So much "connecting" centers on our problems in the hope that someone can make them go away. True connecting centers on the spirit within us, that awakened capacity to experience God.

Our misdirected and overdone emphasis on vulnerability sometimes rewards people too much for sharing honestly about life's difficulties. A renewed focus on what the gospel makes possible—an actual, felt, enjoyed relationship with God—would help us redefine vulnerability as a willingness to discuss whatever is getting in the way of our relationship to God for the purpose of deepening that relationship, not necessarily removing the problems.

Connecting that focuses on the lesser battles of life, such as the struggle to overcome personal injury and to experience emotional freedom, inevitably breeds cultlike arrogance. When this is done within Christian community, God is not so much *enjoyed* as he is *used* to help us explain our dilemma and get a handle on things. When done within the more serious-minded Christian communities, God becomes more of a puzzling enigma than a heavenly Father, more a fickle sovereign than a loving

Lord, more a scrutinized mystery than a trusted friend, someone who is thought about more than worshiped.

It's time for the people of God to enter the primary battle we're all fighting, to connect with each other not about our problems but about our desire to know God. The great danger, if we attempt it, is that we will see how bloody the battle is and quickly distribute Band-Aids and aspirin.

Friends who have lost two much-wanted children to miscarriages and who remain childless have told me how well-meaning Christians have tried to help. One lady delivered an impassioned lecture on God's sovereignty with her beet-red face several inches from my friend's. Several have wagged their heads in sincere sympathy. Not many have explored their struggle to relate well to God in the middle of their heartbreak.

If we are to enter the battle for people's souls, if we are to connect with their longing to relate well to God and with their struggle to do so, if we are to follow the Holy Spirit's lead as he ignites our passion to know Christ, then observing several principles might help.

- *Start with one or two people.* It's just like sharing the gospel. We can (and we should) pray for the world, but we must talk with our neighbors.

Ask God to burden your heart with one person, maybe two, three at most, whose battle you will enter. Realize that your spouse is fighting that battle. So are your children. Without knowing what it means, resolve to enter the battle for their souls. Write down their names in your journal. Begin praying that God will move in their hearts to allow you to join them in their struggles. Don't push. Pray.

- *Keep in mind that solving people's problems is really a secondary battle where you may not be able to help. The primary battle is to know God well.* Don't get so caught up in people's problems that you lose sight of a simple truth: Every problem is an opportunity to know God better. Think more about how people's problems are influencing their relationship to God; think less about how you might be able to help them solve their problems. Don't confuse secondary battles with the primary one.

- *Let people know that you're struggling for them, that you've entered the battle for their souls to more fully experience Christ.* Listen to the apostle Paul: "I want you to know how much I am struggling for you . . . in order that [you] may know the mystery of God, namely Christ" (Col. 2:1–2).

After God revealed himself to Kep in the aftermath of his difficulties in college, Kep moved to Texas. In spite of a wonderful community that faithfully discipled him, his path toward maturity took a few wrong turns. He began dating a lovely girl who was not a believer.

We met her, liked her, enjoyed her—and were scared to death. Was this a ploy of Satan to encourage compromise in a young believer? Would Kep place his affection for this girl over his commitment to honor God in the choice of a mate? The battle was raging.

I wrote him a letter. I told him I was in the battle for his soul, that I was praying every day that his inclination to trust God would guide his decisions. I said that his enjoyment of this girl and the fulfillment he experienced with her mattered less to me than his faithfulness to Christ.

I went so far as to suggest that I thought it possible Satan was using this young woman (without her awareness) to divert him from the good path he had recently chosen. With no planning on my part or Kep's, the girl happened to see the letter I had written, and, completely out of character for her, read it. She was so offended, she broke up with our son. Strange how God sometimes works.

Who in our lives knows how much we're struggling for them? And are we struggling more about their relationship with Christ than about their financial welfare or resistance to sin or career choices or relational success or health problems? All are good and legitimate matters for prayer and assistance, but all are secondary to their need to experience a deeper, sweeter, longer taste of Christ.

- *We must listen with eager interest, willing to enter whatever doors are opened, even a little, and hear what is shared without retreating.*

Years ago, when I first taught a course in counseling skills, I spoke about "door openers." In conversation, people sometimes drop a comment to test the waters, to see if anyone is listening hard and has the interest to pursue involvement. A door opener can be as simple as, "How are things? Oh, OK—could be better."

A response of, "Glad to hear it. Things are never perfect, but we can't ask for that, can we?" leads the other person to quickly close the door and vow to never open it again.

Another response, such as "How so?" might encourage the door to be opened a little further.

Paul tells us to suffer *with* another member of the body who is suffering, not from a distance (1 Cor. 12:26). And we can hear another's suffering without retreating if we remain focused on what battle we are entering (to find God, not solve problems) and if we believe that nothing can separate one of God's children from his love. There is no obstacle that can stand in the way of knowing God better, if in fact that is the battle we fight, the goal we have set.

- *When we enter, we do exactly that: We enter, with only the thought of companionship, not heroic or expert rescue.*

One of my mentors, Chuck Smith, told me that he had scheduled a visit with each of his two grown sons. "It may be my last time with my boys before I die," he told me. Chuck was approaching the last stages of advanced cancer.

I immediately asked, "What will you tell them? What will you talk about that you want them to understand before you die?"

He looked puzzled. "Well, nothing really. I'm expecting we'll probably watch a football game together—maybe we'll hold hands as we watch it. I just want to be with them."

I learned something that day. My inclination to say important things that will change people's lives has more of the flesh in it than I realized. Chuck understood what it meant to simply be with someone, to connect with a deep desire both to enjoy the connection and to whet their appetites for enjoying its source.

My doctors are helping me fight my physical battle. Are we helping each other fight our deepest spiritual battles? It begins by entering the battle with interest, compassion, perspective, and godly purposes. It's time to connect over matters more pressing than our problems. We must join together in our mutual battle to relate well to Christ.

CHAPTER 16

Developing a Vision

I *performed reasonably well* through my first five years of formal education. I can't recall the woman who herded me through kindergarten. But I clearly remember my first grade teacher. I didn't like her.

The kids she thought had average ability were placed at yellow tables. The smart kids sat at red ones. She told me to sit at a green table.

Mrs. Detweiler retired the year after she taught my second-grade class. I was Miss Webster's pet in third grade. When the safety patrol came to "arrest" me for throwing stones at the school bus, Miss Webster wouldn't let them take me away. "Larry wouldn't do such a thing," she huffed. She was wrong.

Fourth grade with Miss Vanaman was uneventful. Then, in fifth grade, my life took on a new direction. (Just having a direction was new to me at that age.)

Mr. Erb, fresh out of college, was possessed by the romantic idea that each child was a unique bundle of potential waiting to be released. He never made the mistake, however, of letting us think for one moment that specialness included the right to be pampered. We worked hard. Mr. Erb had a tough, no-nonsense approach to handling a couple dozen squirmy ten-year-olds.

But he liked us. More important, he believed in us. He thought about what we could become.

One day, about a month into the school year, Mr. Erb called me to his desk. "Class, you're dismissed for recess. Larry, I want to see you for a minute before you leave."

"Uh oh," I thought. "What have I done wrong?"

Mr. Erb looked intense. "Sit down, Larry."

I sat down.

"I've noticed you like words. I've been thinking about that. Larry, one day you could be a writer. Here's what I want you to do. For the last fifteen minutes every day, when I give the class a chance to start on their homework, I want you to take this dictionary"—he handed me a book thick enough to serve as a doorstop—"and find a word you don't know and use it in a sentence you make up. Then you bring that sentence to me and we'll discuss it. OK?"

That was the beginning of my writing career. From then on, through high school, college, graduate school, and into adulthood, I heard a gentle whisper in the back of my mind, "You could be a writer."

That whisper had power. Why?

A year later, I made a diving catch at third base, jumped up, and threw out the runner trying to score. My coach walked over to me and said, "Hey, you might be a ballplayer."

Why did those words stir nothing more than a good feeling and a few Walter Mitty-like fantasies? I had fun dreaming of pitching a no-hitter in the World Series at Yankee Stadium or covering third base like Brooks Robinson, but that's all it was—fun.

Mr. Erb's comment did more than just provoke a few daydreams. It released something. His words sounded strangely familiar, like the echo of a sentence I had heard before. They reached something in me that was already there.[1]

The truth is I think I *had* heard those words before. Is it possible that, from my earliest days, the Holy Spirit had been breathing that same thought into my soul, whispering it to me even in my mother's womb? Could it have been part of his plan to arrange for someone else to say the same thing so that in the mouths of two or three witnesses the idea would be confirmed?

We are not mere mortals, with a chance beginning and a chance ending and a flurry of pointless activity in between. We are meaningful players in a cosmic drama, intended to know that more is going on beyond what we can see. God has "set eternity" in our hearts, and although we cannot fathom "what God has done from beginning to end" (Eccles. 3:11), we sense that the events of life are heading somewhere and that we can get on board or stay seated on the bench.

God has placed his Spirit in charge of directing the story and equipping the players for their parts. By his decision, writing a few books was included in my script. I am free to pursue other interests or to cooperate. If I cooperate, I am lifted up into the stream of his purposes, and my yearning to be a part of eternal things is satisfied. I become one with my destiny.

And it began, humanly speaking, with Mr. Erb.

I wonder what more could be set in motion by visionary words from sensitive members of our community? What could parents say to their children, husbands to wives and wives to husbands, friends to friends, and shepherds to those entrusted to their care? "Consider what a great forest is set on fire by a small spark" (James 3:5). That passage refers to the damage caused by evil words, but the reverse holds as well: Visionary words can release enormous good. "The tongue has the power of life *and* death" (Prov. 18:21).

Something big is waiting to happen that our words can arouse. David was aware that God had been involved in his life from the beginning. "All the days ordained for me were written in your book before one of them came to be" (Ps. 139:16). Paul saw himself and other Christians as the work of a skilled craftsman, as literally God's work of art (Eph. 4:10). We are wrong to not believe that God's Spirit is at work in us and has been from the day we were conceived, that he has been whispering his intentions to us from that moment. As someone put it, "God, help me to believe the truth about myself, no matter how beautiful it may be."

Mr. Erb repeated something God had already said. That's why his words had power, and that's what I mean by vision. When we suggest to others what they one day could be, that suggestion is a *vision* if it echoes what the Spirit has already been saying.

We must clearly understand that a vision for someone is not something we make up or merely something we would like to see happen. Visions are discerned; we don't create them. When the doctor announces, "It's a girl!" he is not deciding the baby's sex, he is happily acknowledging what someone else has decided. That's the first thing we must understand about vision.

The second is this: A vision calls forth what is there. It arouses possibilities we hadn't considered.

I wonder what Gideon felt when the angel greeted him with these words, "The LORD is with you, mighty warrior" (Judg. 6:12). To that point, Gideon had never fought a battle. How did the angel know he was a strong fighter? It was a vision.

And a rather improbable one at that. Gideon was hiding from the enemy when he was addressed as a mighty warrior. The angel's words were like someone greeting a bumpy brown sphere, smaller than a billiard ball, with the words, "Hail, mighty oak tree." If we can see the life within the acorn, we can then see its possibilities.

What happened inside Moses when God spoke to him from the burning bush and said, "You're the man! Go deliver my people from Egypt." Forty years earlier, Moses would likely have replied, "Good choice! You've got an eye for talent. I'm well connected; I'm a powerful leader and a great speaker. Let's get started. Here's my plan!"

But, after four decades of desert living away from all the action, with memories of a bungled effort to free his people, Moses had lost his confidence. In his estimate, he was badly underqualified for the job. Just the idea of returning to Egypt filled him with anxious doubts. Like a movie star well past his prime, Moses couldn't picture himself heading up a cast of thousands.

It was at that point, with his confidence stripped, that God called him to a vision of what he could become. From his earliest days, Moses was under the protection of a God who was preparing him for his part in the drama. When he heard God say, "I am sending you to Pharaoh to bring my people the Israelites out of Egypt" (Exod. 3:10), did he hear a bell ring he had heard before? We're told that Moses persevered "because he saw him who is invisible" (Heb. 11:27). Did he have an unrelenting but for years vague and obscured sense of destiny? When God announced his plan, did Moses say, somewhere in his heart, "Yes, I am the man. This is what I am to do. I cannot—and I do not want to—escape this call."

As soon as we enter the battle for someone's soul, our very next step is to *think vision.*

- How has God built this person?

- What is he wanting to release through all the joys and heartaches of this person's life?

- What is right now being released?

- What strengths does this individual have that, if surrendered to God, could powerfully advance the kingdom?

- What potential remains unrealized because of undealt-with weaknesses?

- How does this person uniquely bless me?

- What does that tell me about the character strengths that God is specially weaving into the fabric of this individual's soul?

The more natural route is to *think problems.*

- What is wrong with this person?

- Where is this individual's sin and damage and hurt?

- How can we smooth out the bumps in this person's life, first by exposing the problems we see and then by figuring out how to deal with them?

- What don't we like about this person and how should we help him or her deal with it?

When we think problems rather than vision, we are quickly overwhelmed. We end up facing too many problems, some that would disappear on their own if we thought vision instead.

Thinking vision is determining your destination before beginning a trip. No sensible person plans a trip by first checking the map of the entire country to see which bridges are out and which roads are closed.

We decide where we're going and then evaluate what problems might get in our way. It would be silly to sit in Philadelphia and worry about road construction en route to Florida if we're heading for Vermont. Fix the destination, and then you'll know what difficulties require attention.

Our culture assumes we all want to reach the goal of good feelings, self-fulfillment, and the freedom to do what we want. We're therefore encouraged to fuss over problems that a better goal would make irrelevant.

For example, if a husband decides he wants to provide his wife with a strength in which she can rest, he will evaluate his own insecure feelings, not as a problem to be solved, but as an opportunity to develop and display deeper courage. He will no longer fret about how weak he sometimes feels.

But if his goal is to feel good about himself, to enjoy a sense of his own manly adequacy, then those same insecure feelings become an obstacle that must be overcome. Now he'll talk about his insecurity too much with his wife and friends and, when they get sick of it, with a therapist. And he will resent his wife when she fails to affirm him. All because he is heading in a wrong direction.

A godly vision lets us ignore lots of problems that a selfish vision requires us to focus on. We need to think *vision* not *problems.* And we need to think *godly* vision not *selfish* vision.

Communities must learn to connect with the uniqueness already stamped into people's makeup by the Holy Spirit and to envision what the Spirit has designed people to become.

Think of it this way. One day, a long time ago, the Trinity decided to create a kind of being that could enjoy the depths of the Father's kindness. They hatched a plan that would allow these beings to actually share in that kindness and to thereby reproduce among themselves the community that the Trinity had always found so delightful.

When they met to discuss that plan, I wonder if the Father said:

> "Son, when you become a human being, I will give you a glory you don't have now. You will then have an unprecedented opportunity to let people see what I'm like, an opportunity that until you live down there as one of them you cannot enjoy. When they watch the way you talk to prostitutes and business cheats, when they see the way

you suffer and handle abuse, they will get a clear glimpse of what I'm like and a vision of what they could become."

"Father," the Son might have replied, "I'll use that opportunity well. And it will be a delight to make you known. When I return to your side after they kill me, I'll give each one of my followers a similar opportunity. I'll give them the glory you will have given me so they, too, can reflect your character to one another. When I'm back home, I'll leave behind a community of people who will carry on the work of revealing your irresistible kindness to others."

And then the Spirit spoke: "No one will ever reflect the Father as you will. But from the moment a new image bearer is conceived, I'll start molding the raw material I have to work with into a person who can uniquely reveal something of the Father and advance his purposes. I'll see to it that nothing happens to your followers that interferes with my design. Everything, even the difficulties they cannot explain, will work together to enhance their opportunities to make you known.

"And then, when the archangel calls them all home to be with us, millions upon millions of individually crafted people, a numberless host of unique persons, will combine like facets on a diamond to shine like the Son."

"Father," again the Son spoke, "my deepest joy will be to represent you to your children and to receive their worship. And then I will sit down at your right hand as everyone bows before your throne. My joy will be complete when I hear our people sing:

'To him who sits on the throne and
to the Lamb
be praise and honor and glory
and power,
forever and ever.' (Rev. 5:13)

"The plan is good. Son, prepare to die. Spirit, set eternity in every heart you create and, as soon as they are conceived, begin whispering your intentions for their lives into their souls. And then, Spirit, inspire the few who listen to you well to repeat to the others what you've already said. That will help them hear you a little better."

Since that time, I wonder how many scores of people have lived and died without ever hearing someone repeat to them what the Spirit has already said. How many have lived their entire lives without a vision of what they could become, without knowing how they were designed to uniquely reflect the Father's character, without thrilling over a glimpse of how they could more closely resemble Jesus?

When we live without vision, the events of life become a patternless sequence of random circumstances with neither purpose nor meaning. Childhood abuse becomes nothing more than a monstrous problem to be overcome on the way to feeling better about ourselves. It is never seen for what it is, a dreadful opportunity to experience the healing power of Jesus and to be more closely drawn into his heart.

Dysfunctional backgrounds are reduced to psychological riddles to be explained, to puzzles with a thousand pieces that must be put into place if we are to overcome the damage we've suffered. Without a vision of what God is up to, difficult experiences from long ago (or today) cannot be viewed as doorways into profound trust and meaningful prayer, as opportunities to be exploited on the path to knowing God and making him known.

My paternal grandmother spent the last six or seven years of her life blind. As a teenager, I once asked her, "Grandma, what's it like to be blind?"

With eyes that saw more than sighted people ever could, she looked at me and said, "Oh, Larry. I can pray so much better for you now than when I could see. Blindness cuts down on the distractions."

She had heard the Spirit's whisper that she was born to pray. And I caught a glimpse of Jesus, the one who prays for me all the time. He had given my grandmother the glory the Father gave him, the opportunity to reveal the character of God. She used it well.

I wonder if someone once said to her, "Laura, I think you were called to pray. The death of your husband when your four children were little, your years of unrelieved poverty, the spiritual indifference of your oldest son, and now your blindness: It seems to me that God wants to draw you so close to his presence that your prayers will become the outpourings of his heart."

"Larry, you could be a writer."

"Laura, I think you're called to pray."

Two statements of vision, two sets of words (one actual, the other imagined) spoken by mere humans that sounded familiar because they had already been whispered by the director of the eternal drama.

Let me say it one more time: *A vision we give to others of who and what they could become has power when it echoes what the Spirit has already spoken into their souls.*

We connect with others when we enter the battle for their souls and when we envision what God may be doing in their lives. Let me mention a few implications of this understanding of vision that might guide us in developing a vision for someone else's life.

Implication #1. *A Spirit-inspired vision sometimes includes an idea of what a person could do, but it always centers on who that person could become.*

Ken, our younger son, began his college career with a declared major in psychology. It never clicked. In that area, he is not a chip off the old block.

But he is a chip off another block and a good one. During the middle days of his college career, Ken and I one day lunched with Richard, a successful and talented financial consultant and also a close friend.

Richard was explaining some new investment strategy to me, a topic that fascinates me as much as counting the blades of grass in my lawn. I noticed Richard's attention shifting away from me toward Ken. My yawns may have been partly responsible. But so, too, was Ken's keen interest.

I heard Ken ask a few questions that would never have occurred to me. I asked Richard, "Is he asking good questions?" He replied, "Oh yes. Excellent questions." And then he good-naturedly added, "Far better than any you've ever asked."

I turned to Ken. "Maybe you're built to think about this kind of thing."

Today, Ken is a highly knowledgeable and effective financial planner. He actually likes to study economic projections and stock trends. How else to explain it than the Spirit's craftsmanship? I certainly had nothing to do with it.

But my vision for Ken goes deeper than handling people's money wisely and ethically. Certainly that. But I also see an eager passion in this unique image bearer to understand basic Christian foundations for living life and to communicate those foundations to others. He thinks logically, precisely, analytically. If I suggested he write poetry, he'd smile and resume reading his *Wall Street Journal.* If I open a discussion about a biblical perspective on wealth, he warms quickly to the subject.

My vision, though, goes deeper still. I envision him as a patient man, a man who responds to the ups and downs of life without requiring things to be different. I envision him relating with Christ so intimately that his soul remains calm in any storm, anchored in the awareness of God's presence, and that his tender heart is increasingly released toward his family and friends, perhaps not poetically but nonetheless genuinely.

A vision from God may involve the practical side of life (forget psychology; major in finance), but it always centers on matters of the heart, on issues of character. The Spirit intends people to recognize Christ when they meet Ken.

Implication #2. *A Spirit-inspired vision for someone reliably creates anguish in the heart of the visionary.*

After forcefully calling the Galatians back to the gospel, Paul referred to them as his dear children and said, "I am again in the pains of childbirth until Christ is formed in you" (Gal. 4:19).

None of us still on earth is where the Spirit has designed us to be. We all have farther to go on our spiritual journey than we've already come. And the possibility of serious failure never ends till we're home. To care about someone's spiritual maturity will always involve suffering.

Only in heaven will love create no pain. To love someone now means that we desire their highest good. And Christians know what that is: to love God with all our heart and soul and our neighbor as ourselves, to know God and his Son Jesus Christ, to become like Jesus. Our highest good is to relate well to God.

But that doesn't always happen. To desire a sure thing, like heaven, brings joy. To passionately want what may not occur provokes pain.

Listen to Paul speak about his countrymen, about Israelites who did not believe that Jesus is the Messiah: "I have great sorrow and unceasing anguish in my heart. For I could wish that I myself were cursed and cut off from Christ for the sake of my brothers, those of my own race, the people of Israel" (Rom. 9:2–4).

Every parent knows something of that pain. Every true friend does as well. We have no greater joy than when the people we love walk with Christ. But we know that wrong turns may be taken. And when they are—when a son leaves his wife, when a friend's ambition releases more ruthlessness than love, when a husband frequents adult theaters—we hurt. Badly.

A Spirit-inspired vision for someone engages us in spiritual warfare. Final victory is guaranteed, but along the way, temporary setbacks or serious defections create levels of anguish that reduce us to prayer. It's easier to want less for people we love. Good visions hurt.

Implication #3. *A Spirit-inspired vision is necessarily the product of spiritual discernment. Without ongoing fervent prayer, our vision for others becomes self-serving.*

I wonder how many born writers were steered toward baseball by athletic fathers. How many perfectly good dentists, do you suppose, became mediocre preachers because of zealous Bible teachers who taught that some vocations are more sacred than others? No doubt more than a few gentle encouragers have worked hard to build organizations to prove to someone that they could lead when a behind-the-scenes job would have better released them to touch dozens of discouraged people with hope.

We all carry with us an image of a perfect spouse, a perfect child, a perfect parent, a perfect employer, employee, or friend. Our definition of perfect typically highlights what that person could do that we would most appreciate, that would do us the most good.

If a husband, for example, were to read this chapter and then, without serious prayer and self-examination, come up with a vision for his wife, the effects could be disastrous.

> Honey, my vision for you is that you become more content with the money we have and with the decisions I make on how to spend it, that you exercise more self-control in your diet (self-control is one

fruit of the Spirit), and that you stand faithfully with me in all the trials I face.

We all have a vision for the important people in our lives. And most of them are better left unstated. Without prayer and a growing sensitivity to God's Spirit, our vision reflects arrogance and becomes rudely imposi-tional: "Here's what I think you should do."

When we start thinking about our vision for someone, we must first develop a vision for ourselves as abandoned to God, demanding nothing for our satisfaction, committed only to furthering God's agenda. It is important to realize that we may never develop a truly selfless vision for others until we're older, perhaps much older, maybe till we're blind grandparents who can pray without distraction. Until the desert and darkness and difficulties and the damage we cause have helped us mor-tify our flesh, we may not hear the Spirit who has already spoken his words of vision to us. It might be a good idea to speak our vision for others with a great deal of humility, so much so that we're surprised when we do speak the Spirit's mind.

Implication #4. *A Spirit-inspired vision sometimes develops best when the one about whom we're forming the vision is farthest from God.*

When someone we love is doing well on all obvious fronts, it is natural to relax, to go off duty, to let our prayer life slack. Parents, especially, attend to the signs of storms or sunny days. A flat hello in response to her phone call and a mother's heart is filled with worry. But a bouncy greeting, which may mask more troubles than a flat voice reveals, puts a mother's heart to rest. We so want to believe things are fine that, on insufficient evidence, we sometimes believe they are.

Until the affair comes out in the open. Or a grandson is arrested for dealing drugs. Or a wife is diagnosed with clinical depression.

When the facade is ripped away and we have to believe that things are bad, we tend to respond in one of two ways. *Either* we lament, despair, talk about it to our circle of friends, frantically seek help, and pray for God to do something, *or* we retreat to our prayer closet to develop a vision of what God could do.

Option one makes us desperate. It wrings us out and leaves us emotionally limp. Option two draws us into the council of God, it deepens our dependence on him, and, as our wrong dreams shatter, it allows us to hope again, this time in Christ.

> God, how have you designed her? Right now she is so far out of your plan. What have you been whispering to her heart that neither she nor I have yet heard? How can I stay involved in a way that lets her know I am jumping up and down with delight over the uniqueness you have stamped into her soul? God, help me to never give up on her but to always hope in you, until the day I die, when everything will be clear.

The brightest visions sometimes come in the darkest nights.

Implication #5. *A Spirit-inspired vision is less concerned with practically moving someone in a good direction and more concerned with catching a glimpse of what could be.*

The glimpse itself is motivating. It arouses the life of Christ within us. When we preoccupy ourselves with how we can help someone get to a good place, the vision blurs. We forget where we're going while we try hard to get there.

Counseling theories would do well to focus more on their ideal of emotional health than on either pathology or treatment technique. Thinking less about the path to our destination allows the Spirit the freedom he demands to move us along any way he chooses.

But that's not our inclination. We are inveterate problem solvers. We depend on people who know what to do to help us reach the goals we set. We want expert help, not to determine which goals are worthy, but to affirm the goals we already have and to help us reach them.

Spiritual communities focus more on vision: What could be? What is God doing in our lives? What might he do through us to bless others? Whatever map we need to find our way becomes clear after we let the Spirit tell us where we're going. Friends who develop visions for others that come from God know that only God can bring them to pass. So they pray and love and listen. *Something is released in them that God can use to move people toward the vision.*

Connecting begins when we enter the battle for someone's soul. It continues as we prayerfully envision what Christ would look like in that person's life. It climaxes when the life of Christ within us is released, when something wonderful and alive and good pours out of us to touch the heart of another.

Releasing the energy of Christ—that's my final topic in this book.

CHAPTER 17

Releasing the Energy

I've had the high privilege of speaking to people I deeply love when they were experiencing significant struggles. Never have I felt less like a psychologist plying my trade and more like a dependent Christian earnestly wanting to pour out the energy of Christ than at these times. As I speak with someone during personal crisis, maintaining professional objectivity seems worse than irrelevant; it blocks the release of power. I must enter the opportunity with biblically informed and Spirit-guided subjectivity, with passion arising from the deepest places within me. Cool detachment would violate what is alive and good. It would interfere with forming the connection that can bring healing.

When someone I love is hurting and perhaps caught up in the devil's schemes (how I hate the devil!), I pray this prayer:

> Lord, only your life touching this person's heart can do what needs to be done. My skill, my cleverness, my knowledge add up to nothing if your life is not the energy controlling everything I do. Father, I'm overwhelmed by the awful possibilities this person is facing. I can feel the terror in my bones. But I also taste the peace beneath the terror of knowing the power of your grace. Reveal your Son through me that I might be a powerful instrument for good in your Spirit's hands.

We spent some time this morning in Sunday school class praying for several especially difficult physical problems. Margaret's husband is nearing death after a long battle with brain cancer. He is forty years old. Mark suffers from a strange neck disorder that was x-rayed last week. He will hear the results in four days.

Debbie has two bad wrists and one bad knee, each of which has received several surgeries. Yesterday her good knee went bad. Lynn's elderly parents are facing an assortment of medical challenges that could soon claim both their lives. Larry (not me, another one) has an ankle that will be operated on this week. I just passed a kidney stone and can again be more concerned with a yearlong battle with intestinal problems and dehydration.

Al led us by naming each request then giving us a minute or two to pray silently. When I got up to teach, I asked how people had prayed and whether they had made their requests without doubting, as James tells us to do when we face various trials (James 1:6).

We agreed that it is right to ask our Father to fix necks and repair knees, but we also admitted that we couldn't pray for physical healing with unwavering confidence. We've all had too much experience with prayers for recovery that have not been answered as we wished. It struck me that I can pray with more confidence for successful ankle surgery than for cured cancer because (and I'm not comfortable admitting this) the former might occur whether God directly intervenes or not. For advanced brain cancer to disappear, God must perform an obvious miracle.

And that doesn't happen too often in our day. With Gideon, I ask, "Where are all his wonders that our fathers told us about?" (Judg. 6:13). I have no confidence that the prayers of fifty people in our class, or even a million people across the world, will reliably persuade God to cooperate with our wishes. We publicly praise him for his sovereignty while privately complaining that he can seem so independent, so aloof from our heart's desire, so, well, stubborn.

Until we realize what he's up to. Then our perspective changes and worship becomes real. Since Eden and until Christ returns, God has entered a battle with a vision for what he intends to accomplish. The battle is not to improve our circumstances, to supply us with money, to protect us from suffering, to keep us safe from pain and struggle, or to quickly fix whatever problems develop in our bodies. We are encouraged to pray for all these things, but we must always finish our prayer with that wonderful caveat that in our immaturity we find so annoying: if it be thy will.

Isn't it his will that his children enjoy the blessing of healthy bodies and pleasant circumstances? Apparently not. At least not in this life. In his old age, Peter said we were called to suffer well. He later admonished us to not be surprised when painful trials come our way as though something unexpected were happening (1 Peter 2:20–21; 4:12).

God will one day wage war against every reason for tears, and he will win. But for now he is fighting a different battle that, as it is successfully fought, leaves plenty of reason for tears. Until we go home, we can count on God to lead us into battle against *soul disease.* That's the war he is waging today. And that's the war he wants us to fight along with him.

The battle plan is simple. We are to help one another mortify the flesh, which short-circuits the power of the world and the devil, and to vivify our spirits, which arouses the good urges within us that, when released, make us more like Jesus.

When he chooses, God can as easily reverse cancer as fix necks. But he gives us no reason to count on him to do so. To pray for physical healing with confidence is really presumptuous. It reflects an arrogant demand more than humble faith. We can ask him to cure our bodies with confidence that he *can,* but we can ask him to heal our souls with confidence that he *will.*

When the class shared how they prayed that morning, Mark's dad said, "I prayed that my son would trust Christ more completely whatever the outcome with his neck." Someone reported their prayer for Margaret was that she would know God's presence and become filled with gratitude as she watched her husband deteriorate from cancer, not gratitude for the pain but rather for God's eternally good purposes and his tender involvement through it all.

As I listened, it became quietly clear: We really are in the battle for each others' souls. It's a good community. We do what we can to assist with the more practical matters—meals are brought in, rides to the hospital are provided, prayers are offered for physical healing—but we realize that the most good will come as we struggle to help each other become more like Christ.

But that battle is a difficult one. We're not as inclined to talk about it. It's far easier to say, "My good knee gave out. Please help me get into the car and pray the doctor can repair it," than to admit, "I'm losing perspective. Life is so unbearably hard right now, with no prospect for improvement, that I want to quit. I don't care about anyone else. I'm sitting in a muddy puddle of self-pity, and I feel mean, cold, and mad. And desperate. But I don't want to feel that way. Can you help?"

What would we feel if we heard a friend say that? Time to call the pastor or refer to a Christian therapist.

We readily make known our upcoming surgery, but we're reluctant to reveal our fears: "I'm scared to death I might lose my job. And I'm taking it out on my wife. I've lied to her that I have disability insurance. I don't. I know it's irrational, but I'm furious at her for everything. I've even considered leaving her. My life is a mess. Can you help?"

We feel adequate to pray for physical healing, but we feel inadequate to help with each other's soul battles. We can enter the battle by listening and caring. We can envision what Christ could do, and we hold out hope that self-pity will yield to faith and resentment will be replaced with love.

But when it comes time to actually speak helpful words, to say things that might make it happen, we plead ignorance. Someone, we realize, needs to address the jealousy and bitterness and lust and terror that have gained a foothold in people's souls. Someone should be talking with these people, someone trained to understand how traumatic histories relate to current emotional problems. Someone is needed who knows what to look for, how to probe, and what to do with whatever surfaces.

Caring friends *can* enter the battle. They can even provide vision and resolutely believe in what troubled folks could become. But someone must perform verbal surgery, someone with knowledge and skill must deal with the root problems.

That's what our culture assumes. And that person, we further assume, is a trained therapist. Qualifications to help consist of degrees completed, extensive supervision, and official recognition of professional competence. Pastors and friends and family members can only do so much. We can walk with a friend as she is wheeled down the corridor, but when she is taken into the surgical theater, we wait outside while the professionals work. We're with her in the battle, we steadfastly believe that the Spirit can do miracles in her soul, but to actually perform the surgery, to talk powerfully and healingly with her, well, that's out of our league.

But maybe not. Could it be that training in counseling has become so necessary and valued because few Christians know what it means to release the energy of Christ from within them into the souls of others? If the battle is against soul disease, and if the real disease is disconnection caused by sin that leaves the person starving for life, isn't it our calling to supply life to one another, at least a taste of it that drives us to run to the source?

During a call-in radio show where I was discussing these matters, someone phoned to comment: "I appreciate Dr. Crabb's emphasis on the healing power of community. It's wonderful to be loved and heard and prayed for. But sometimes we need counseling."

And, in a sense, the caller was correct. We need more than people who will enter our battles and give us a vision of what Christ will do. We need folks who can talk to us wisely and sensitively and meaningfully about our deepest battles, our most painful memories, and our secret sins. My contention, however, is that the person best qualified to engage with us at those levels is the person most filled with the energy of Christ. That person may or may not be a trained professional. The energy that fills a truly qualified helper includes far more than "mere" compassion, it involves engagement that goes miles beyond listening skills; it offers probing wisdom and life-giving words that provide more than the promise to pray, gestures of support, and bits of advice.

Read the Gospel accounts of Christ's life. He understood what was in the minds of people. He knew how to touch the desire for something better in an immoral woman's heart and when to expose her bad choices. He was perfectly adequate in dealing with grieving people who were frustrated with him for not showing up before their loved one died. He didn't get into a power struggle with the servants of Jairus who told him, "Your daughter has died. Don't bother the master any further." He simply ignored them and told Jairus to believe. With craftsmanlike artistry, he handled an impulsive fisherman with a perfectly timed rebuke, a poignant glance, gentle but unrelenting exposure, and soul-nourishing affirmation. Peter became a wise shepherd of God's people. And Jesus was not at a loss to deal with quarreling companions.

If we understand what is available to us through God's Spirit, if we appreciate the life of Christ within us and properly value the development and release of his energy, we will feel inadequate to touch a loved one's soul only if that energy is not powerfully working in us, not because we lack professional training.

And those of us involved in counselor training would center our efforts on identifying, nourishing, and releasing the energy of Christ in all our students.

> Dear Lord, people I love are not doing well. My husband, my wife, my son, my daughter, my parent, my friend are struggling with weary, sick, discouraged, stubborn souls. Their response to life's hardships is fleshly. God, use me to awaken their spirits by pouring your life through me into the hard ground of their hearts. Let the water of life penetrate the thick crust and nourish the good work your Spirit is now doing in their souls. Nothing will help except an experience of life. Pour out that experience through me.

In order to release the energy of Christ within us, we must understand that the deepest reality within our being is the life of Christ. Our task is to identify that life and to consistently nourish it till it becomes stronger than every other impulse within us, until we doubt but more firmly believe, until we worry but more quietly trust, until we feel inadequate but more passionately depend on the Spirit to guide us. That's what it means to vivify our spirits.

And we must learn to distinguish between what at any moment may *seem* most real and what *is* most real. We will have butterflies when the couple we are discipling informs us they are considering divorce, but the deeper reality is that there is a power within us that could turn the tide and restore a marriage. We move forward with that confidence.

Releasing the energy of Christ comes down to one profoundly simple procedure: *We learn to say what we most genuinely want to say as we live in the presence of Christ.* That is our freedom. No longer do we scramble to come up with wise words that fit a theory of counseling, instead we trust the Spirit within to impress us with what to say and do at any moment. We simply give ourselves, whatever is most deeply within us, discerning what is fleshly and must not be given and releasing what is spiritual and can be powerfully offered to another.

What I've just said can be badly misunderstood and misused. Let me discuss what is necessary to wisely discern the life of Christ within us and to recognize its many counterfeits. Then I'll share a few implications that might guide us in releasing only what is good.

When their little girl was five years old, Peter Kreeft and his wife were informed by the doctor that the child had a large brain tumor. Peter's immediate inclination was to ask a dozen questions: How big is it? Is it benign? When will you know? What are statistics in cases like this?

He later wrote in his journal: "Strange how the mind fixates on physical details in order to handle the unhandleable. When we can't handle truth we handle facts."[1]

A friend's father recently died. After the funeral, well-wishers wanted to know if he left insurance. Was health insurance adequate to cover the medical costs of his prolonged dying? Will your mother have enough money to live on?

He answered honestly, no, things are a financial mess. To which the well-wishers replied, "What a tragedy!" My friend wanted to scream, "No! The tragedy is that my father died!"

When we can't handle truth, when what is most terribly true is too disturbing to face, we run to facts surrounding the truth and hide behind them. It gives us something to do, something to think about that we can manage, something we can at least pinpoint.

There is, of course, some functional value in this tendency. The parents of a little girl need their wits about them to make rational decisions and not terrify their daughter with out-of-control emotions. Sons of widowed mothers must come up with plans to handle financial challenges. Surgeons cannot afford to dwell on the truth that the small head they are about to cut open belongs to the precious daughter of frightened parents. They rightly concentrate instead on the facts of good surgical procedure.

Sticking with the facts is a good thing to do when allowing yourself to be overwhelmed by a devastating truth would get in the way of doing what is best. A steady, skilled hand holding the scalpel is more important than a compassionate heart.

However, when we shift battles from responding to physical disease or circumstantial difficulties to fighting for someone's soul, things are exactly reversed. Healing power in that battle consists of pouring out what is most profoundly alive within someone's heart. Connecting matters more than coolly applied skill and carefully studied knowledge. Detached technique has no place in healing a soul.

We must get in touch with what is deepest within us and offer that to the other. To do that, to actually know and experience the richest parts of our redeemed souls, we must be overwhelmed by the truth: This is my son who is making bad choices, this is my husband who is far from the Lord, this is my friend who is suicidal, this is my life that is filled with horrible abuse.

Only then will we be forced to wrestle with our foundations. Only then will the reality of our faith, the new birth, and God's character become apparent. We find God only when we need him. When we handle a tough situation by strategizing an effective response, our dependence on God is token.

And that's our tendency. What should I do? How can I explain what's happening? What theory can best guide me as I seek to understand this person's problem and helpfully respond? When we ask those kinds of questions, we get so caught up in analysis that we never experience what God is doing within us.

Picture it simply. Here's the truth, the frightening reality of what is happening in the life of someone we love.

Disturbing Truth

If we respond to our terror by quickly thinking through an effective response, we lose the opportunity to touch what is alive and powerful and good within us.

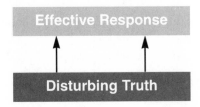

Suppose instead we allow ourselves to be devastated by the truth, to be overwhelmed with the sadness and pain it creates. We will soon sense our inadequacy to change what needs to be changed, we will face the truth that a troubled, hardened, foolish heart needs to be impacted and that only the Spirit of God can make that happen.

At that point we will have only two choices: Yield to despair or find God. If we begin looking for God, we will then enter a whole new battle. We will be thrown onto God, we will long to see his face, we will wrestle with our fears and doubts in his presence, we will seek him with all our hearts.

Because he promised to let us find him when we seek him with a stronger passion than we seek anything else (such as solutions or relief), we will find him. We will find him in his Word. After a long fall through darkness, we will land on the truth of his eternal, almighty, and loving character, and we will believe he is always up to something good. And we will find him *within* us in the form of holy urges and good appetites and wise inclinations that reflect the character of Christ.

In more familiar language, the energy of Christ is released most fully when we most completely come to an end of ourselves.

Surgeons have legitimate confidence in their ability to operate well. Good mechanics experience a relaxed sense of adequacy when a motorist describes the strange noises coming from under the hood. In their work as skilled professionals, they have no need to come to an end of themselves because they truly are adequate in themselves to fix things.

But without Christ's energy flowing through us, we are not adequate to restore a soul to godly functioning. When a parent speaks with a child about a significant struggle, nothing less than the power of God is required to heal that child's soul. If we learn what it means to struggle with the

energy of Christ and experience the reality of that energy working powerfully through us (Col. 1:29), we will know the indescribable joy of being
an instrument in God's hands for healing a human soul.

The route to power lies in embracing the disturbing truth and moving
beneath it to discover the exhilarating truth of God.

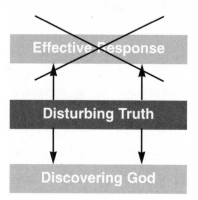

A father hears that his married son is having an affair. The truth rips
him apart.

Does he strategize or weep? Does he immediately plan his response,
consult with people whose advice he respects, and move forward to
handle the problem? *Or* does he let the weight of the news crush him so
thoroughly that he discovers the foundation of God's peace beneath his
heartbreak?

If he frantically searches for facts, if his focus is on devising an effective response, he runs the risk of releasing the energy of his flesh. I *will*
handle this:

- I will build my city.

- I will light my fire.

- I will whitewash my walls.

- I will dig my wells.

But suppose he moves in a different direction. Suppose he retires to his
prayer closet; weeps openly with his wife then joins hands with her to

pray; presents himself naked before the Lord, perhaps wracked by guilt, resentment, and fear; and mortifies his urges to control the situation. Then he will eventually discover what is alive and terrific and strong and clean within him.

He will emerge from fighting this battle with the calmness of trust, with brokenness over his demanding spirit, and with confidence that God can work through him to powerfully battle the enemy on behalf of his son. And he will emerge with a spirit of grace and intuitive wisdom.

When he speaks with his son, he will speak like Christ, without judgment but with morality, without bitterness but with grace, without despair but with hope, without distance but with love, without superficiality but with discernment. He will become a tool under the Spirit's control who uses the glory given him by the Son to reveal the Father's heart.

Nothing matters more than releasing the energy of Christ as we speak with people we love, especially when those people are in the midst of trouble.

Facing the truth of what is going on in people's lives, no matter how ugly or sad, is a necessary path to discovering what is deepest within us. That truth then prompts us to nourish the life we find, to sanctify ourselves for the sake of others (John 17:19). And then we're freed to speak genuinely rather than skillfully in our efforts to arouse the work of God in another person's life.

Because the life of Christ is the deepest reality within our souls, we can pour out that life into another when the problems we encounter drive us to our foundations, to the final truth lodged in the center of our souls. When we discover what is most central in our hearts, we can trust it. The inclinations most deeply imbedded within us are from God. They must be identified then nourished to become stronger than the bad urges. But as they grow, we can more freely release the energy that Christ has placed within us as we battle for someone's soul. We will probe wisely, rebuke in a timely and gracious way, ask questions about things that matter, and offer direction that arouses a person's spirit to trust and obey.

Several important implications of this concept should be noted:

Implication #1. *Nourishing the energy of Christ within us requires that we study, pray, serve, and worship. Trusting our hearts must never be understood to mean that we can bypass spiritual discipline.*

Christ is the theme of Scripture. He spoke to his contemporaries with a thorough knowledge of the Old Testament that was gained through the disciplined study expected of every Jewish boy.

We can do no less. Speaking out of our impulses is dangerous business unless the impulses are carefully informed by a growing, rich, biblical understanding, unless they remain firmly within the boundaries laid down by the objective text.

If someone says, "I think you should divorce your husband. He is not fulfilling you as a woman. You deserve better," we know that person is not speaking with the life of Christ because the words violate Scripture.

Similarly, without a vibrant prayer life, we dare not trust our impulses. And, as we give ourselves in sacrificial service to others and abandon ourselves in meaningful worship, we draw nearer to God's heart and the good urges within us are nourished.

Implication #2. *Releasing the energy of Christ is enhanced by thinking through biblical categories for understanding people, their problems, and what can be done to help.*

Powerful helping involves biblical discernment into the nature of people's problems. For the past thirty or forty years we have assumed that developing the needed discernment is best accomplished through specialized counselor education, most often in academic institutions outside the church.

It's time to consider another possibility. If ordinary Christians with no licensed credentials have the power within them to heal souls through connecting, then perhaps the church should view it as its responsibility, as a normal part of its educational program, to equip people with a biblical understanding of change, to actively prepare people more meaningfully to connect.

Soul care has more to do with waiting on God to impress us to move in certain directions than with logical analysis. But those directions do not reliably develop in a vacuum of understanding. To know what to say to a man addicted to pornography or a woman filled with self-hatred requires a *well-informed subjectivism*, neither a detached objectivism nor mindless subjectivism. We need the wisdom that can be gleaned from biblical content and from those who have thought long and hard about these matters.

Of course we need training. But if helping people has more to do with connecting than technique, with pouring out the life of Christ than interpretive skill, then perhaps the community of believers should be equipping themselves to more wisely connect by offering the appropriate training.

Implication #3. *Models for helpfully speaking to people have most value for those who are least experienced.*

I envision a training program to help people speak with the wise, informed energy of Christ that includes charts, lectures, books, supervision, and critique. I want people to have some reasonable clue about where to move when someone admits a loss of interest in life.

But I also envision a decreasing conscious dependence on the biblically guided models we create as we become more seasoned.

Michael Jordan, arguably the best basketball player to ever play the game, was gathered with his teammates around the coach in the final seconds of a close contest. Coach Jackson sketched the plan. He turned to each player and gave them specific instructions. When he came to Michael, he put down his clipboard and said, "Michael, you just do whatever it is you do."

At first we must learn some fundamentals of helpful talking (don't give advice too soon, avoid power struggles, listen for what is not being said that may be important), but eventually the Spirit tells us to do what comes most naturally.

This book is a call to connect, to work with people as they struggle to kill their bad urges and pour into them what is most alive within us to help them arouse their good urges.

We've thought about a variety of concepts that hopefully can stir us and better equip us to connect:

- The *Trinity,* the eternally connecting community, a pattern for our relationships.

- The *gospel,* God's provision of forgiveness from sin, a future of perfect community, and the freedom to connect more deeply with God, others, and ourselves.

- The *New Covenant,* that wonderful arrangement established by God through which he actually plants the urge to be good within our hearts. We no longer need to merely exhort people to do what's right or work on people to fix what's wrong; now we can connect with them to release what's good.

- God wants us to *mortify the flesh,* the source of all those bad urges that try to convince us we'd be better off yielding to them, and he helps us destroy our bad urges by arranging for us to spend time in the desert, to walk in impenetrable darkness, to encounter unexplained difficulties, and to face the damage our selfishness causes others.

- The *glory* given to us by Christ, empowering us to reveal the Father's heart as we enter the battle for someone's soul, develop a vision for what they could become, and release the energy of Christ within us by pouring our own deepest selves into others and so arousing their urges to do good.

In telling Kep's story at the beginning of this book, I said, "Something came out of me that cut through Kep's hardness and reached the tender part of his soul with healing power." In further describing that time shortly after my son was expelled from college, I added: "A power was released through me that had never been as fully released before."

I then asked, "Could it happen in your relationships?" My answer, and I hope yours, is yes, it could.

On so many occasions, however, something different from healing power comes out of us. When children disappoint us, when friends worry us, when spouses keep their distance, we back away from meaningful engagement. Often we do little more than moralize or, if things seem too complicated, we suggest professional help.

In many interactions with people, we *build our cities* by looking good, fitting in, impressing someone, or veiling impatience or boredom with social courtesy. Or we busily *light a few fires:* arguing a point, feeling defensive, or enjoying someone's agreement too much. Sometimes we *whitewash flimsy walls,* reminding ourselves that our lives will probably be spared significant tragedy because we deserve certain blessings, we take our faith quite seriously, and we're rather vital to God's purposes. Most often, we *dig our wells,* doing whatever it takes to feel the way we want to feel or, if that's not possible, arranging to feel at least a bit better.

It's all fleshly energy with no power for good. And it makes connection impossible. Whatever community forms is shallow, fragile, perhaps satisfying for a while but always ready to disintegrate.

It could be so different. I'm learning more about what it means to release the energy of Christ, whether with my son during a crisis, with a friend who's struggling, or with my wife in the normal everydayness of life.

There is a wonderful energy in each of our hearts, placed so deeply in us by the Holy Spirit that no failure or heartbreak can dislodge it. Our spirits are *alive* with the actual life of Christ.

But they need to be vivified, to be aroused, nourished, believed in, valued, and invigorated.

Hard times will do it, if we let them. A determination to pray, not out of mere duty but out of a desire to know God well, is requisite. Learning the Bible, through reading it ourselves and profiting from good teachers, must be a priority.

Facing the truth about our lives and not retreating behind bunches of facts will carry us deep into our own souls, from where Christ's life is waiting to emerge. When we need him, we'll find him. We'll recognize him as the most wonderful person we've ever met; and then, sometimes without trying, we'll act just like him.

We'll ask our sons how we can help, and lives will change. We'll smile at our spouses with a new kind of appreciation and kindness, and they will soften and move toward us. We'll listen to friends confess moral lapses and an awareness of grace will fill us and flow into our friends, who will then pursue God as never before. We'll see people whom we know don't like us, and we'll sincerely wish them well without feeling self-righteous.

When we enter the battle for someone's soul, when we envision what the Spirit has long ago planned for that person's life, and when the energy of Christ pours through our words into the other person's soul, we'll connect! Healing will happen.

Can you hear the Godhead as they watch? I can hear them saying with one voice, "The plan is working. But they haven't seen anything yet. *It's almost time!*"

EPILOGUE

Getting *started on anything worthwhile* is difficult, whether a diet, an exercise program, or a campaign to make new friends. It's no different with connecting.

Now that you've read the book, I hope you're finding within yourself a desire to experience a deeper level of relationship with someone, a level where substantial healing takes place.

To help you get started, I want to suggest that you select one person in your life and write a letter with the theme of "My Vision for You." You might reread chapter 16 to make sure you don't simply write out your personal (and maybe selfish) "wish list" of how you want another to change. Remember that a good vision is one that the Holy Spirit thought up long before you and has already been whispering to the other person. Your job is to audibly express what he has been wordlessly suggesting.

Several years ago, it struck me that Paul had a clear vision of what Timothy could become. If I had the chance to ask Paul, "What is your vision for Timothy?" I think he would have put down his coffee, leaned across the table, and with concentrated passion said, "Oh, let me tell you. God's at work in that young man. I see him boldly proclaiming Christ, humble but unapologetic for his youth, willing to suffer anything for the privilege of knowing Christ, and . . ."

With some embarrassment, I realized I had never carefully prayed about a vision for the people I most love. That's when I decided to write a letter to my wife. She read it and immediately wanted to write her vision for me.

We thought it might encourage you to think vision, perhaps to write similar letters to someone whose battle you want to enter, if you could read our letters.

We therefore decided to include this epilogue where we reproduce our vision letters to each other. Rachael tells me my letter to her touches her as deeply as I know hers touches me.

Dearest Larry,

My vision for you is to see you peacefully settled—settled in who you are in Christ and in his call upon your life. You are one of the best things that has happened to me. We have a long history: nine years of dating and thirty-one years of marriage. I know you; you're godly, generous, kind, thoughtful. In our forty years together, I have seen the Lord's hand upon your life. I've followed you in all the calls he has placed on you (not because I'm a doormat but because I know you seek to be in the center of his will).

As your wife, I want to be there with you. In the beginning of our marriage, you were settled and confident, maybe with the confidence that belongs only to youth; but in these last few years, and with a clear new call on your life, I have seen you as never before: self-doubting, unsure, questioning, tentative. I have a vision for the good God is working in you through these hard times, but I don't like seeing you in that unsure state of mind. I want to see you emerge from this darkness, this desert, with a peaceful settledness, with a firm aware-ness that God's hand is on you. (I trust my vision for you is not to make my life easier, though it would be easier for me if you were settled.)

So I'll paraphrase Paul from Galatians 4:19 to say what's most deeply in my heart:

> My dear husband, for whom I am again in the pains of childbirth till Christ is formed in you, till you clearly sense his leading and pres-ence; Larry, I'll hold your hand as we go through the labor pains together toward your being peacefully settled in his call. I respect you and love you as no other man. And I have a vision for you that time only deepens.

Love,
Your Rachael

Epilogue

Dear Rachael,

I met you in the middle of your four years of sexual abuse. I first dated you the year it ended. All I knew about you then was that you were pretty—and that there was something about you I saw in no other girl. Forty years later, I still think you're pretty, and I still see something in you I see in no other woman.

But now I think I know what it is. I see in you a beauty that has survived a thousand assaults, half of them from me, a beauty lodged so deeply in your soul that no power can dislodge it. But there is a power that can suppress it.

Sometimes I see you feel insecure, wondering if anyone really loves you, worried that if anyone could see all of you they'd find more to criticize than enjoy. I've helped make you feel that way, and my failure and your pain break my heart.

I want to love you with a powerful tender love that lets you feel how Christ feels about you, that will give you the courage to believe that no matter who criticizes you, no matter how hidden you feel, you will know that God delights in who you really are and that any who has his eyes will feel the same way. I see in you a terrific thing.

My vision for you is that you rest, never that you be one ounce less spontaneous, friendly, outgoing, and involved, but that you quietly relax in the knowledge that I will always move toward you on behalf of God, that you are a deeply enjoyed woman with something beautiful to give that gets more beautiful the older you get.

I want to love you so well that you rest. I want to honor your uniqueness, prize your individuality, treasure your feelings and thoughts, respect your opinions, and be there for you in every moment of life, so that you're released more and more to give to this world all that is within you that has the aroma of Christ, and to more deeply rest in your Father's tender arms.

That's my vision for you. Rachael, you are the most alive woman I've ever met, the most remarkable woman I know. I have no higher calling than to reflect Jesus to you. I love you.

Larry

APPENDIX A

The Talking Cure Does Not Belong Only to Professionals

A s I finish this book, I feel the need to pause and take a deep breath. The thoughts I'm putting in print feel radical, out of step with culture, and therefore easily caricatured as simplistic or fanatically soft-headed. To some, I fear, they will sound like the ravings of a captain who has been too long at sea returning to port and announcing that the world is flat.

Doesn't every Christian know that obedience is the center of Christian living? Every parent, pastor, and policeman knows that giving orders and enforcing consequences (Christians call it accountability) has a place in persuading people to be obedient. Where do I get the idea that connecting is more central than obedience?

And doesn't every enlightened Christian realize that when obedience becomes difficult because of psychological problems, counseling by a trained professional can be helpful? Haven't we established that professional counseling can overcome emotional disorders and restore people to fruitful lives of obedience and service? Why would we think ordinary Christians can cure psychological disorders any more than we assume they can treat kidney disease? Some problems require professional help. Isn't that clear to every modern person? Let's think about that.

Professional counseling is a specialized form of talking that we assume only highly trained people can practice. But that assumption is not well supported by the evidence. Talking to people about your problems is, of

191

course, a good idea. It often helps. The majority of people who talk to therapists find it helpful. But the ingredient that makes professional talking helpful may have little to do with professional training; there is reason to suggest that caring, intelligent people, with much less training than is required to become a professional counselor, can achieve equal and sometimes better results when their efforts to helpfully talk are carried out as part of healthy community.

Think of a person who is struggling with a problem, perhaps a dad worried sick about his rebellious teenage daughter, a young man who wakes up once or twice a week with panic attacks that convince him he is about to die, an older woman recently widowed who cannot bear the ache that won't go away, a youth pastor who scares kids and offends parents with his temper, a senior pastor who likes to counsel young, attractive women in the privacy of his office, a young woman who binges and purges but doesn't do it often enough to call herself bulimic, a middle-aged psychologist who shifts his direction midstream and sometimes wonders whether it's worth the hassle.

What do these people need? Probably a variety of things might prove helpful, but most would agree that it would be good if they had someone to talk to.

A prominent leader in the field of psychotherapy, Dr. Hans Strupp, recently looked back over fifty years of research on the effectiveness of psychotherapy and came to this conclusion:

> The simple incontrovertible truth, it seems to me, is that if you are anorexic or depressed or if you are experiencing difficulties with significant people in your life, chances are that you will feel better if you talk to someone you trust.[1]

Let's begin simply. We have a hurting person who wants help, and someone worthy of trust who wants to help. We all agree it's a good idea for these two people to talk. That means they will get together and exchange words.

The hurting person will share what is troubling him. The helping person will try to say helpful words. They will attempt to connect.

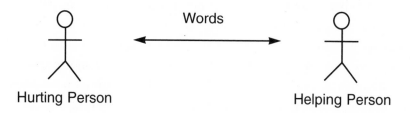

The question the helping person will necessarily ask is, "What makes words helpful?" or, "What are helpful words?" Should helping people listen, offer advice, provide reassurance, quote Bible verses, pray, exhort different behaviors, empathize, probe into forgotten memories or buried pain, interpret the meaning of certain actions and tie them to internal choices and external influences?

The question is, "What words will help?" But to answer that question, we must first ask another: "What needs helping that words can do something about?" Are there repressed emotions that *uncovering words* can surface? Are people indifferent to their responsibilities and therefore in need of *rebuking words*? Are they confused about what to do and looking for words of wise counsel, for old-fashioned good advice? Do our problems stem from forgetting that God cares and that a few other people do too? Are *encouraging words* the most helpful? Or are people empty and in need of receiving what words can pour into their souls? Are *pouring words* the answer?

In defining what is wrong that words can do something about, our culture has made a pivotal decision. For nearly one hundred years, reasonable people have agreed that beneath the hurts, pains, and struggles of life there often lies something called "psychological disorder."

Although that term has been defined in a thousand ways, the general idea is that something has been damaged in our internal pattern of processing ourselves and our lives and that the damage needs to be fixed. Many theorists speak of a sense of self, a personal identity, that has been damaged by abandonment or rejection or abuse. Others speak of persistent habits of thinking and acting that were formed to meet difficult circumstances that no longer exist.

The theories are varied, but it is commonly agreed that only folks trained in psychology (the study of how people function), psychopathology (the study of what goes wrong and why), and psychotherapy (the study of how to use words to fix what's wrong) can speak with real helpfulness to hurting people. Other folks can encourage and support, but only therapists know how to fix what's wrong. Therapy, it is assumed, is as different from a layman's effort to help as antibiotics are from chicken soup. Laymen can support, encourage, and maybe even offer direction, but they have no power to heal. That power belongs to professionals, and it comes with training.

Helpful talking has been professionalized. Hurting people have become patients or clients. Their job is to put words to their problem, to describe their concerns and cooperate in discussing what their therapist thinks is important to talk about.

Helping people who become therapists or counselors use words that their trained understanding leads them to assume will do some good. Licensed professionals, it is assumed, can do what unlicensed helpers cannot do.

Now the picture looks like this:

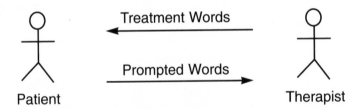

It is commonly observed that patients tend to fit the words they say into their therapists' theoretical molds. Patients of Jungians notice archetypes in their dreams. Patients of cognitive therapists eventually report irrational automatic sentences that run through their heads. Patients of psychoanalytically oriented therapists remember forgotten traumas and project what they feel toward their parents onto the therapist.

The effect, of course, is that therapists' theories are "confirmed" by clinical experience and their understanding of change validated when patients improve. But a wealth of studies have discovered that different therapies seem to work equally well. Although consumer satisfaction among therapy patients is high, the level of satisfaction has little to do with what kind of therapy the therapist practiced.[2] It is hard to avoid the conclusion that what helps is focused, well-meaning conversation about problems. But how does that help? And *why* does it help?

In the treatment/repair model, where therapists treat patients who have psychological disorders, words are believed to be helpful because they effectively address root problems that nonprofessionals do not understand. Symptoms arising from repressed pain disappear when *interpretative words* are spoken with theoretical precision and artful timing. When deep shame is the culprit, *words that surface* the unreliable source of the shame may help, along with *reminding words* that affirm an individual's unique value. When hidden idolatry is the trouble, *probing words* that expose the sinfulness of the action may effect the needed repentance. And these words, it is assumed, must be spoken with artistic impact and scientific precision, something that a professional is trained to do.

Generally, the treatment/repair model depends on revealing words to do the job. Their power lies in exposing whatever has been denied.

Now we can refine our sketch a bit further.

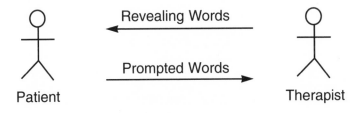

Treatment/Repair Model

This way of thinking, so thoroughly embedded in Western culture and significantly absent in Eastern thought, has influenced the way Christians think about personal growth. Whether it's therapy narrowly defined or recovery from addictive disorders through the healing of self-hatred or deliverance from an alien evil that has gained a foothold in the personality, the hurting person is afflicted and the helping person is skilled at revealing the affliction and curing it. In this approach, the cure involves *doing something to a person*. It has little to do with *releasing something in a person*.

The major alternative to the treatment/repair model is the exhortation/accountability model. In its general form, it is the model that most conservative evangelicals live by. When a problem arises, the task is not to look for its cause in some psychological disorder; it is rather to determine what biblical principles of living are being violated, to exhort conformity to those principles after confession and repentence, and to follow up with accountability to see whether the good intentions were carried out.

In this model, the hurting person becomes not a patient suffering from psychological disorder but a violator of God's authority. The helpful person assumes the role of God's representative and, on the authority of Scripture, provides not therapy or treatment but instruction, first teaching the violator what needs to be done, then securing a commitment to do it, and finally following up on whether the commitment was honored. The model can be applied harshly or gently and there are variations to it, but its essentials are well described by the words exhortation and accountability.

We can sketch it this way:

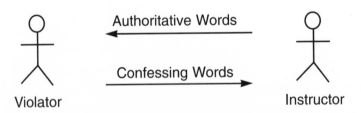

Exhortation/Accountability Model

Because the treatment/repair model is more widely accepted in our therapeutic culture, I want to spend more time suggesting why its understanding of helpful words is inadequate. The only comment I wish to make about the exhortation/accountability model is that it assumes the root problem always lies with a wrongly active will that must be firmly redirected. Communities that try to help people change according to a rigid interpretation of this model are known more for their pressure than for their graciousness, and they defend their reputation as consistent with the legitimate demands of holiness. The law, it seems, has become the point rather than a good escort to Christ. They don't make it past Moses. This approach, rather than releasing what God has already put within someone, requires that people conform to standards that are external to them.

My concern, however, is more with the thinking that psychological disorder lies beneath many of our problems and that helpful words can most powerfully be spoken by a professional, by someone who will fix what is wrong in a person. Because that thinking effectively puts ordinary Christians out of business as healers of the soul, I want to evaluate whether the assumptions beneath the treatment/repair model stand up well under scrutiny, including scrutiny from its proponents.

Psychotherapy has developed such an aura of mysterious scientific respectability—with its complicated jargon, its technical feel, and its private character—that most people are intimidated when they meet a psychiatrist or psychologist at a social gathering. "Oh my gosh, I'll bet you can see right through me."

I used to enjoy maintaining that image by flippantly responding, "Therapy is hard work. If you're not paying, I'm not thinking."

But the mystique loses some of its glow when you know a little history. Consider the following.

In 1895, Freud stumbled on the idea of a talking cure. Some problems, he discovered, simply went away when people talked about them. His creative mind immediately went to work to explain what he discerned. How does the human personality work? Why does talking to people help? Can I figure out which words help more than others? What do certain kinds of words actually do that's good?

The idea of a talking cure caught on. Good thinkers began to take seriously Freud's report that special kinds of conversation between two people had the power to relieve problems that neither medicine nor religion could touch. They asked many of the same questions Freud had asked and further developed the ideas he was coming up with, in some cases departing radically from them and designing theories of their own.

But a core idea emerged. Unhealthy psychological processes that the patient did not recognize (and did not *want* to recognize) lay hidden beneath visible problems and were, in fact, their source. These processes, set in motion by contact with unhealthy people, developed into organized and firmly fixed patterns called psychological dynamics, which infected the psyche much as bacteria infects the body. Verbal treatment that consisted of three parts was required to cure the disease: (1) figure out what psychological processes lay beneath the presenting concerns; (2) decrease the patient's resistance so that the unconscious dynamics became conscious; (3) work through the unhealthy patterns triggered by earlier relationships until the patient replaced them with a healthier, more chosen approach to handling life.

Before long, a new profession emerged. Specialists in helpful talking introduced themselves to the public as psychotherapists. They offered to treat problems they theorized lay beneath people's struggles in living, problems they labeled as "psychological disorder," which only psychotherapy, a unique way of talking to people, could cure.

New schools of thought flourished, each with its own gurus, jargon, and training regimen. It wasn't until halfway through the twentieth century that serious thought was given to whether psychotherapy for psychological disorder was living up to its billing.

In the mid 1950s, British psychologist Hans Eysenck rocked the world of therapy by providing evidence that people improved as much without psychotherapy as with it. His research implied that people who just kept on living (in community? perhaps talking to friends about their problems?) tended to deal with their concerns as well as those who made a therapist their primary community for helpful conversation.

His conclusions have since been widely discredited because of weaknesses in research design, but his unnerving observation struck a chord. As often happens with new ideas, when the initial excitement wears off, people begin to wonder if the idea is as good as it first appeared. For the first time since its beginning in 1895, psychotherapy came under serious critique. Did it really do any good? And was it doing any good that untrained caring people couldn't equally well provide?

For the second half of the twentieth century, in the midst of ongoing theory development, the professional world took a hard look at the validity of what they were offering to the public as a specialized talking cure.

Hans Strupp, the research scientist and therapy practitioner quoted earlier as saying that talking about problems is a good thing to do, went on to comment on helpful talks:

> Such conversations may be brief or may extend over a period of time, they may occur in a religious or professional context, or they may be conducted by people who have been assigned special roles by society (e.g., shamans) or, as is true of the present time, by specially trained professionals who charge a fee for their services.[3]

This is remarkable. A modern leader in the field of psychotherapy is suggesting that helpful conversations for troubled people can occur in a variety of settings with a variety of people, not just with psychotherapists during clinical sessions. Could the same be said of brain surgery?

He then adds, "The critical feature of all successful therapy, it seems to me, is the therapist's skillful management of the patient-therapist relationship."[4] In other words, *people who are good at relating are people whose words will be helpful.*

This raises the obvious question that Strupp himself asks, wondering about "the kind of training that might be required or whether training is expendable."[5]

Another professional therapist reports that "literally hundreds of studies . . . suggest that psychotherapy works better than nothing. What is not so clear is that psychotherapy works for the reasons specified by the theory."[6]

Is the American Psychiatric Association then wrong in listing more than 360 different ways to be mentally ill, implying that in each case there is some form of psychological disorder that requires a specialized form of helpful talking called psychotherapy? What do we make of the trend to

include more and more problem behaviors as symptomatic of psychological disorder? In its most recent diagnostic manual, the association
listed one hundred more disorders than in the one before it. It is clear that
the professional community of therapists and counselors is expanding
the realm in which its unique services are required.

But at the same time, serious students of psychotherapy are suggesting
that *rich* talking, not necessarily *trained* talking, is helpful. To refer to
Strupp one more time, after asking whether training is really essential
to equip someone to helpfully talk, he concluded that training achieves
three things: (1) it promotes a higher sense of ethical commitment; (2) it
encourages the trainee to better handle a patient's hostility and resistance
without becoming defensive; and (3) it tends to increase a therapist's
human qualities, things like empathy and concern for another's well-being.

A case can be made that training in specific theory and technique is
less important in becoming a good helper than learning to be conscien-
tious, nondefensive, and caring. Engage with patients, honor confidences,
and let yourself actually care when they hurt. Believe in patients, involve
yourself because you really think they could be better, that they are worth
caring about. The evidence from psychotherapy research indicates that
these sorts of things may be the ingredients of helpful talk.

Now our sketch must change.

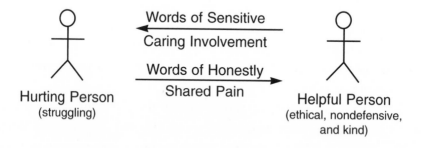

A New Model?

I conclude that we have made a terrible mistake. For most of the twentieth century, we have wrongly defined *soul wounds* as *psychological disorder* and delegated their treatment to trained specialists.

The results for the church have been significant. Three stand out.

1. *We no longer see the church as a place for the substantial healing of personal wounds. Ordinary Christians have been told they have no power to provide real help for deep problems.* Certainly some form of preparation and thought is important in equipping someone to deal with runaway kids, suicidal businessmen, anorexic girls, and sexually addicted men. But we regard relationships, the real business of the church, as having little to do with profound soul care and, in so doing, we have underestimated the power that God has placed within his family. Community could mean far more than it often does.

2. *The work of discipling has been wrongly defined as less than and different from psychotherapy and counseling.* Maybe it isn't. Maybe discipleship, defined properly as caring for the soul, is the reality, and psychotherapy is the imitation. Perhaps husbands and wives should be discipling each other; perhaps parents should be discipling their children, and friends should be discipling their friends. Maybe they can, and maybe discipling (or shepherding) was designed to do what we think only therapists should tackle.

3. *Professional training is thought to be more important in developing the "skill" of helpful talking than the sanctifying work of the Spirit.* If soul care involves pouring something good out of one person into another, if releasing what is good is more central to healing than requiring what is right or repairing what is wrong, then the helper must have something good to pour. Skill in giving matters but not as much as having something to give. A talented doctor with no medicine is not much help. Only God can supply the medicine needed to heal someone's soul.

Our entrenched and growing dependence on professional experts to help us with our problems is one important reason for the crisis of care in Christian community. The effect of that dependence has been to ask less of community than it could offer, to be too easily satisfied when church budgets are met, when conversions are reported, when tensions do not interfere too much with the operation of church activities. We have not yet explored the possibilities of what I could mean to you and what you could mean to me. We have unwittingly encouraged parents to feel inadequate in dealing with their discouraged or underachieving or substance-abusing teens when we could instead help them to see what profoundly believing in their kids could do, what could happen if the energy of Christ flowed out of ordinary untrained parents into their children. We have settled for pleasant relationships when we could be enjoying powerful relationships. Husbands and wives get along when they could be touching each other's souls. Friends are content to spend fun evenings together (and may good old-fashioned "shallow" evenings of fun increase) when they could know the joy of meeting one another as they've never met before.

The community of God can be back in business as the major provider of soul care. The talking cure does not belong only to professionals. It also belongs to ordinary Christians. At least it could—and should.

This possibility raises more than a few important questions, such as:

- Is there a place for the counseling professional? If so, what is it?

- How should Christian community be structured to release the healing potential of its members? Should elders counsel? Pastors?

- Should we train lay counselors?

- What preparation is required for Christians to powerfully connect?

- Are there different levels of connecting?

- What are the limits on what connecting can do? When is it appropriate to refer someone to a trained professional?

In Appendix B, I briefly respond to some of these concerns. It would take another book to adequately deal with all the important issues raised here, but at least some indication of my thinking about them may be in order.

APPENDIX B

Q uestion 1: *Counselors? Shepherds? Friends? Who do we need? Is there a place for the counseling professional? If so, what is it?*

Concerns that are best understood by empirical research are best handled by a qualified professional. Such a specialist's claim to expertise is based on high-level study of relevant research, a growing mastery of its conclusions and implications through formal training and ongoing practice, supervised experience in dealing with the presenting concerns, and credentials granted by an appropriate regulatory body certifying technical and procedural competence in handling a certain range of problems.

Empirically researchable concerns do not fundamentally reflect struggles in the soul, rather they follow relatively predictable patterns in terms of cause, nature, and resolution. They should therefore be treated by trained people who are substantially familiar with these elements and skilled in applying what they know.

These personal concerns fall broadly into four categories:

1. *Those that are caused or significantly aggravated by organic factors and/or can be meaningfully relieved through physiological/chemical intervention.* This category includes psychotic reactions, severe affective disturbances (especially bipolar reactions and clinical depression), obsessive-compulsive disorders (though not proven to have a neurological or chemical cause, they sometimes can be effectively

relieved through medication), attention deficit disorder/ hyperactivity, and some cases of sexual dysfunction (e.g., impotence, orgasmic inability, premature ejaculation).

2. *Those that reflect largely nonmoral processes of learning and conditioning.* I would here include many educational problems (slow learning, poor reading skills, and so on) and related behavioral disturbances (particularly in children) as well as certain anxiety disorders (phobias, panic attacks).

3. *Those that pose significant threat to personal well-being or social order.* Suicidal impulses and antisocial behavior are the two most obvious examples.

4. *Those that represent ignorance of effective technique or understanding.* Such things as marital communication patterns and handling teen rebellion might be helped by experts with extensive experience in family matters. Vocational guidance also falls into this category.

These four categories reflect difficulties with physical, learning, or technique functions. Well-informed diagnosis and treatment is appropriate and often helpful.

Consider, however, the wide range of concerns that do not easily fit into any of the four categories:

- Most personality disorders (narcissistic, borderline, dissociative identity disorders)

- Nonextreme mood problems (mild to moderate depression) and existential despair (often confused with severe depression)

- Relational difficulties (inability to get close to others, most marital tensions, alienating relational styles, anger/impulse control)

- A host of everyday problems, such as insecurity, indecisiveness, superficiality (denial), resentment, worry, many sexual struggles (including perversions and addictions)

These, I suggest, are concerns of the *soul*. Their roots lie in disconnection, in a flesh-driven response to life's disappointments. It is wrong to conceptualize these problems as evidence of a damaged self caused by painful experiences. It is more accurate to see them as the fruit of one's effort to handle life's challenges (finding meaning, experiencing wholeness, relating well, handling sorrow) without God, without honestly facing oneself, and without giving to others. The problem, at root, is the flesh. The cure is the spirit: a new heart that trusts God and perseveres in faith, that equips us to reconnect with God in worship and obedience, with all that is within us, and with the humanity of others.

These problems do not require the services of a trained expert; they require involvement from a wise elder. Kindness from a peer or older friend is sometimes all that is required. Connection is the solution to disconnection.

Question 2: *Do these ideas on connecting carry implications for how professional counselors/therapists should practice their craft?*

Most definitely. Remember, I have distinguished two kinds of problems: those that require the services of a technically trained professional (psychoses, ADD, and the like) and those that represent struggles in the soul. My thinking on connecting has *relevance* to the work of technically competent professionals as they treat empirically researchable disorders, the first kind of problem, but it should never *replace* professional competence.

But, when the presenting concern grows out of soul struggles, I believe that a rich understanding of connecting, disconnecting, and reconnecting (including an appreciation of biblical anthropology, trinitarian theology, and New Covenant blessings) should provide the framework for all helping efforts. I am still involved in the training, supervision, and occasionally the practice of professional therapy, but all that I do in this arena is an outgrowth of my theology of the soul as outlined in this book.

Question 3: *Are you saying that professional counselors are not necessary for handling personal problems growing out of soul struggles?*

Theoretically, yes. But I also recognize that very few Christians value the profound healing possibilities of friendship and shepherding enough to think hard about what that might require. In our culture, we rarely have important conversations about difficult matters with someone who listens and understands outside of a counselor's office.

As long as the resources of community remain undeveloped, professional counselors will occupy a legitimate place. I am arguing that what good counselors do more closely resembles what real friends, wise shepherds, and seasoned spiritual directors do than what we assume technical competence enables. Qualifications to effectively counsel have more to do with wisdom and character than with training and degrees. Wisdom and character should be developed in Christian communities. When it isn't, we turn to educational institutions to provide us with trained, degreed helpers. When these folks are effective, however, it has more to do with their wisdom and character than with their technical knowledge or procedure.

Question 4: *What then should the church do?*

Center on connecting. Focus on what it means to become dispensers of grace, accompanied by wisdom. Develop friends, shepherds, and spiritual directors.

Notice I have spoken more about *communities* than about *churches*. In Western culture, the word *church* rarely calls to mind what I mean by community. More often, church means an organization with numerical and financial goals that have little to do with building real community. For their success, churches tend to require cooperation more than connection.

I see a healing community as a group of people who place *connecting* at the exact center of their purpose and passion—not evangelism, not teaching, not preaching, not missions, not music, not social action, not numerical growth—but *connecting:* connecting with God (worship), others (loving service), and ourselves (personal wholeness). All else is either a route to or a result of connecting. Loving God and loving others lie at the core of God's intention for his people.

When connecting lies at the center of community, priority thought will be given to the issues of community:

- What constitutes *friendship?*

- What does it mean to *shepherd* others, to be an *elder?*

- What is *spiritual direction* all about, and who can do it?

206

A healthy community is built on *friendship*, on people who are committed to the art of caring engagement, an art that only the gospel makes possible in its richest form. It is built on *shepherding*, on people committed to the art of mentoring or passing along hope. Shepherds are simply older friends whose experience allows them to give hope that whatever is happening can be well survived.

Healthy communities also include *spiritual direction*, the art of discerning the deepest recesses of the soul with a sensitivity to what the Spirit is doing accompanied by offering one's presence to another. Spiritual directors need to think about biblical categories for understanding themselves and others. They must immerse themselves in spiritual theology (where truth dynamically impacts life). They will often grow through involvement with their own spiritual director. They will read widely in spiritual classics and good literature and will ponder lessons from life and the arts. And they will learn to recognize and disrupt the evil passions and plans of the flesh while clinging to a vision of what could be released in another's life.

When problems that reflect physical or practical matters of living arise, a healthy community will gladly refer people to professional experts for help. But the community will care for the souls of its people through friends, shepherds, and spiritual directors.

ENDNOTES

CHAPTER 2

1   James Houston, *The Transforming Friendship* (Oxford: Lion Publishers, 1989), 5.

2   As I give one or two sentence snippets of what could be said, I would not want to be understood as believing those are sufficient. Each sentence should be read as representing a lengthy dialogue, perhaps lasting several months.

3   There are cases where the bad was offensive enough to God's purposes that the extreme discipline of death was imposed. Read the story of Ananias and Sapphira in Acts 5. But even here, assuming they were believers, the bad was exposed in a manner that revealed their goodness as they entered heaven. Even Lot, a righteous man, was rescued from the distress he felt living in the midst of filth. See 2 Peter 2:7.

CHAPTER 3

1   Henri Nouwen, *The Inner Voice of Love: A Journey Through Anguish to Freedom* (New York: Doubleday, 1996), xiii, xiv.

2   Nouwen, xiii, xiv, xv.

3   Nouwen, xiv.

4   Henri Nouwen, *Our Greatest Gift* (New York: HarperCollins, 1994), 114.

CHAPTER 4

1   Hans Urs von Balthaser, *Prayer* (San Francisco: Ignatius Press, 1955), 61.

2   Ibid., 60.

CHAPTER 5

1   R. C. Sproull, *The Mystery of the Holy Spirit* (Wheaton, IL: Tyndale, 1990), 90.

CHAPTER 6

1   In this chapter, I introduce the idea of having a vision for someone else. What a vision might look like and how we can develop some understanding of what God has in mind for another person without either dishonoring that person's uniqueness or imposing our preferences will be discussed in a later chapter.

2   This incident is reported in a wonderful book by Rachel Naomi Remen, *Kitchen Table Wisdom: Stories That Heal* (New York: Riverhead Books, 1996), 63–65.

CHAPTER 7

1   In John 17:25–26, Jesus told his father that the central purpose in his coming was to reveal the Father to the world.

CHAPTER 8

1   Jonathan Edwards, *The Religious Affections* (Edinburgh: The Banner of Truth Trust, reprinted 1986), 27.

2   John Owen, *Sin and Temptation* (Portland, OR: Multnomah Press, 1983), 156.

3   Carl Henry, *God, Revelation and Authority* vol. 4 (Waco, TX: Word Books, 1979), 501, 502.

Endnotes

CHAPTER 12

1   Jesus spoke of the *hollow core* of our souls being filled with his living water (John 7:37–38). That's the root meaning of the place referred to in the text with the words *from within him.* Paul used the same words to tell the Philippians about people whose god was their *stomach* (Phil. 3:19). The thought seems to be that if we don't fill our deepest core with Christ's love, that core will become an emptiness, a demanding appetite that insists on being filled with something.

CHAPTER 15

1   Each of these activities is, in fact, strong medicine, but we've come to think of them as spiritual supplements.

CHAPTER 16

1   Twenty years ago, I found out that Mr. Erb was then serving as principal of an elementary school within a few miles of the one that I had attended. I stopped in, unannounced, and gave him a copy of my first book.

CHAPTER 17

1   Peter Kreeft, *Love Is Stronger Than Death* (San Francisco, CA: Ignatius Press, 1992), 114.

APPENDIX A

1   Hans Strupp, "The Tripartite Model and the Consumer Reports Study," *American Psychologist* (October 1966): 1017.
2   "Mental Health: Does Therapy Help?" Consumer Reports (November 1995): 734–39.
3   Strupp, 1017.
4   Strupp, 1022.

5   Strupp, 1017.

6   Steven Hallon, "The Efficacy and Effectiveness of Psychotherapy Relative to Medications," *American Psychologist* (October 1966): 1025.